WHAT?
WHY?
WHAT?
WHY?
WHY?

TIME FOR KIDS
BIG BOOK OF ANSWERS

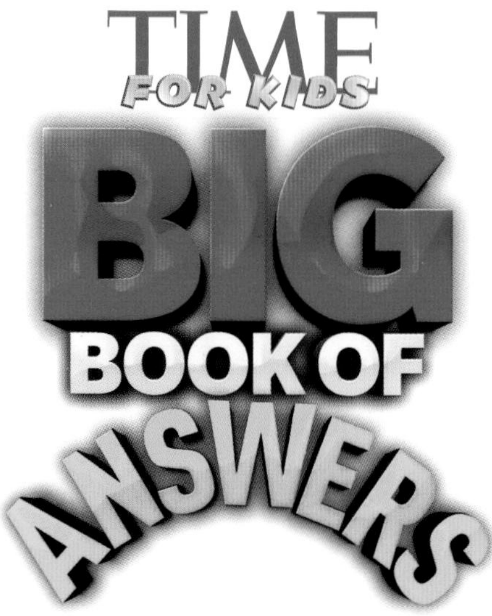

TIME For Kids

Managing Editor Nellie Gonzalez Cutler
Creative Director Jennifer Kraemer-Smith
Project Editor Andrea Delbanco

Created by 10Ten Media

Managing Directors Bob Der, Scott Gramling, Ian Knowles
Creative Director Crhistian Rodriguez
Managing Editor Andrea Woo

Time Inc. Books

Publisher Margot Schupf
Associate Publisher Allison Devlin
Vice President, Finance Terri Lombardi
Executive Director, Marketing Services Carol Pittard
Executive Director, Business Development Suzanne Albert
Executive Publishing Director Megan Pearlman
Associate Director of Publicity Courtney Greenhalgh
Assistant General Counsel Simone Procas
Assistant Director, Special Sales Ilene Schreider
Assistant Director, Finance Christine Font
Assistant Director, Production Susan Chodakiewicz
Senior Manager, Sales Marketing Danielle Costa
Senior Manager, Children's Category Marketing Amanda Lipnick
Manager, Business Development and Partnerships Stephanie Braga
Associate Production Manager Amy Mangus
Associate Prepress Manager Alex Voznesenskiy

Editorial Director Stephen Koepp
Art Director Gary Stewart
Senior Editor Alyssa Smith
Editor, Children's Books Jonathan White
Copy Chief Rina Bander
Design Manager Anne-Michelle Gallero
Assistant Managing Editor Gina Scauzillo
Editorial Assistant Courtney Mifsud

Special thanks: Allyson Angle, Keith Aurelio, Katherine Barnet, Brad Beatson, Jeremy Biloon, Ian Chin, Rose Cirrincione, Pat Datta, Assu Etsubneh, Alison Foster, Erika Hawxhurst, Kristina Jutzi, David Kahn, Jean Kennedy, Hillary Leary, Kimberly Marshall, Robert Martells, Melissa Presti, Danielle Prielipp, Kate Roncinske, Babette Ross, Dave Rozzelle, Ricardo Santiago, Divyam Shrivastava, Larry Wicker

For information on TIME FOR KIDS magazine for the classroom or home, go to TIMEFORKIDS.COM or call 800-604-8017.

Published by TIME FOR KIDS Books,
An imprint of Time Inc. Books
1271 Avenue of the Americas, 6th floor
New York, NY 10020

ISBN 10: 1-61893-150-4
ISBN 13: 978-1-61893-150-4
Library of Congress Control Number: 2015941306

We welcome your comments and suggestions about TIME FOR KIDS Books. Please write to us at: TIME FOR KIDS Books, Attention: Book Editors, P.O. Box 361095, Des Moines, IA 50336-1095
If you would like to order any of our hardcover Collector's Edition books, please call us at 800-327-6388, Monday through Friday, 7 a.m.–9 p.m. Central Time.

1 TLF 15

Welcome

Have you ever wondered why so many people are afraid of spiders? Or where electricity comes from? How about when the computer was invented? Or the difference between a comet and an asteroid? If you're in search of answers to such fascinating questions, we've got you covered! In TIME For Kids *Big Book of Answers*, you'll be exploring the animal kingdom, reaching the far ends of the earth, and then blasting off into space. You'll also learn about cool inventions, great masterpieces, and how the human body ticks. Get answers to the questions you've always pondered—and more!

Contents

Animals

Why shouldn't dogs eat chocolate?

The chemical in chocolate that makes it taste so good, theobromine, exits our body quickly. The body of a dog, however, can't get rid of it quickly enough. It can cause trouble with the dog's heart, digestive system, and brain that can even be deadly. Dark chocolate, which contains more theobromine, can be especially dangerous to dogs.

Why do sharks have so many teeth?

Sharks need extra teeth because they lose so many of them. Their teeth come out easily when they bite into or chew their prey. Their teeth grow in a series of rows, allowing new ones to move up when the old ones fall out. Some shark species can have thousands of teeth during the course of their lifetime.

How do chameleons change color?

Skin: Is green or brown when the chameleon is resting. This helps it blend into the background. Pigments under the skin change the lizard's color, depending on temperature, sunlight, and mood.

Tail: Is prehensile, meaning it can curl and wrap around branches.

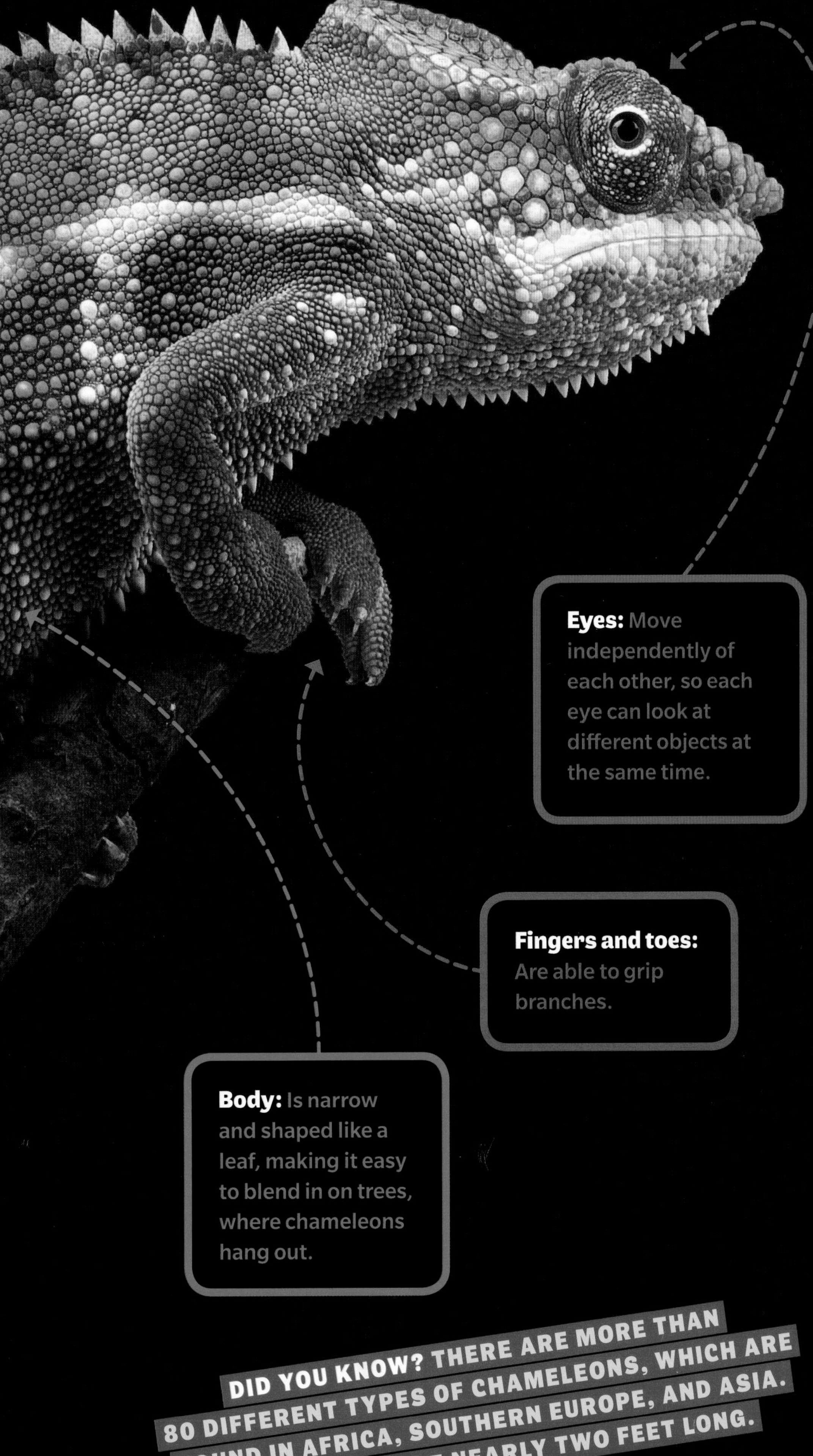

DID YOU KNOW? THERE ARE MORE THAN 80 DIFFERENT TYPES OF CHAMELEONS, WHICH ARE FOUND IN AFRICA, SOUTHERN EUROPE, AND ASIA. THE LARGEST ARE NEARLY TWO FEET LONG.

Chameleons can change their colors in seconds from brown to green to red to blue. Experts believe light, temperature, and mood affect the lizard's color. A chameleon might turn from brown to green to reflect sunlight and stay cool. Or it might become darker to absorb the sun's heat. An angry chameleon can turn dark red or yellow to warn other chameleons to back off.

The secret to this color explosion is skin deep. Under a chameleon's skin is a layer made up of red or yellow pigment (color) cells. Another layer reflects white and blue light. Yet another layer has particles called melanin, which can make colors darker.

Nerve cells direct color cells to get bigger or smaller or cause melanin to spread throughout other layers. If a chameleon is angry, the yellow cells might expand. Various pigments blend to produce different colors. For example, if the yellow cells expand and more blue light reflects upwards, the chameleon turns green. (Mixing yellow and blue creates green.)

What are the differences between ASIAN and AFRICAN elephants?

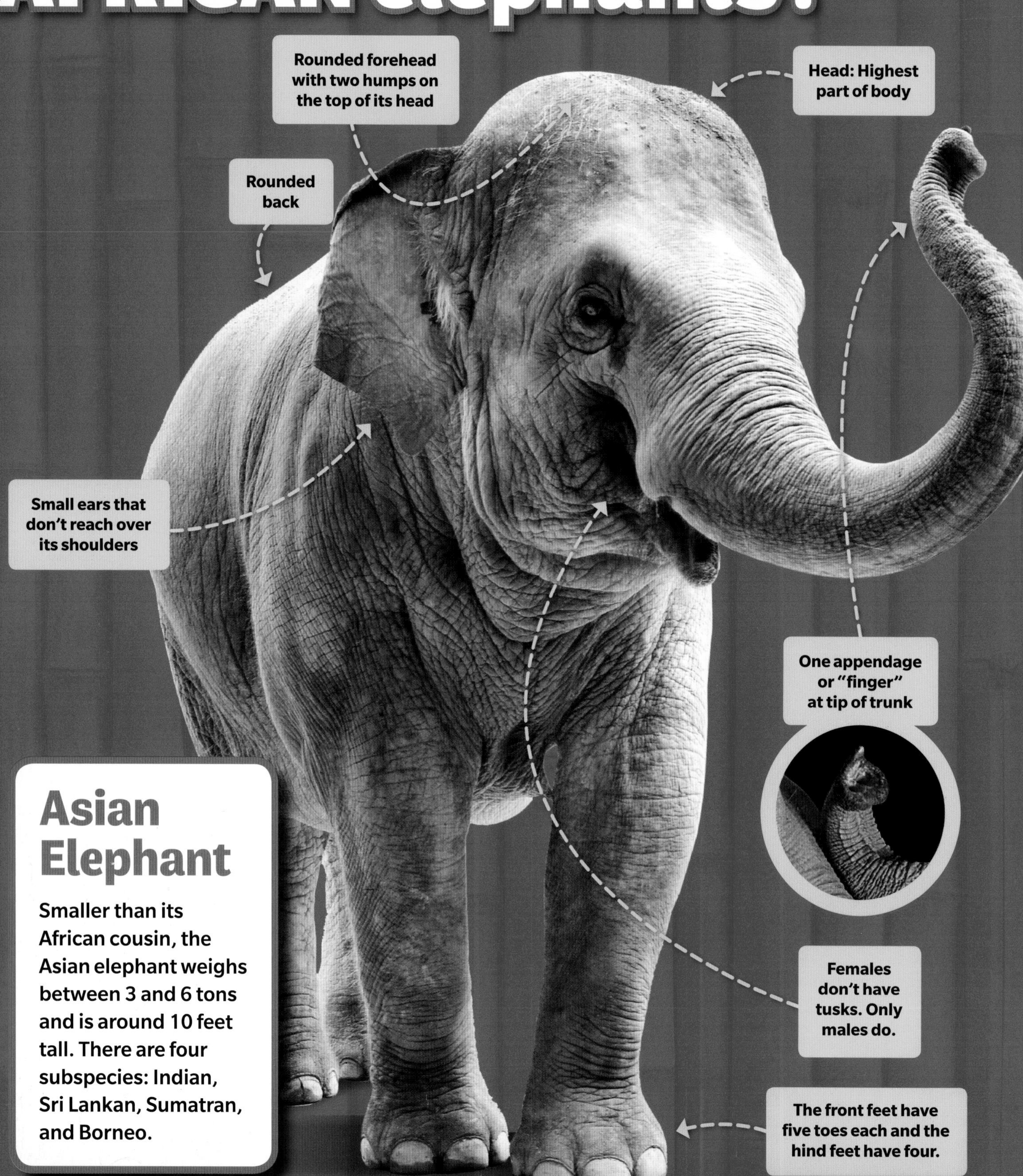

Asian Elephant

Smaller than its African cousin, the Asian elephant weighs between 3 and 6 tons and is around 10 feet tall. There are four subspecies: Indian, Sri Lankan, Sumatran, and Borneo.

To most people, an elephant is an elephant—a big, gray, wrinkly animal with a long trunk. But there are actually two species of elephant: One lives in Africa and the second in Asia. Here's how you can tell them apart.

DID YOU KNOW?
THE SMITHSONIAN NATIONAL MUSEUM OF NATURAL HISTORY IN WASHINGTON, D.C., DISPLAYS THE LARGEST KNOWN AFRICAN ELEPHANT. IT STANDS A TOWERING 14 FEET TALL.

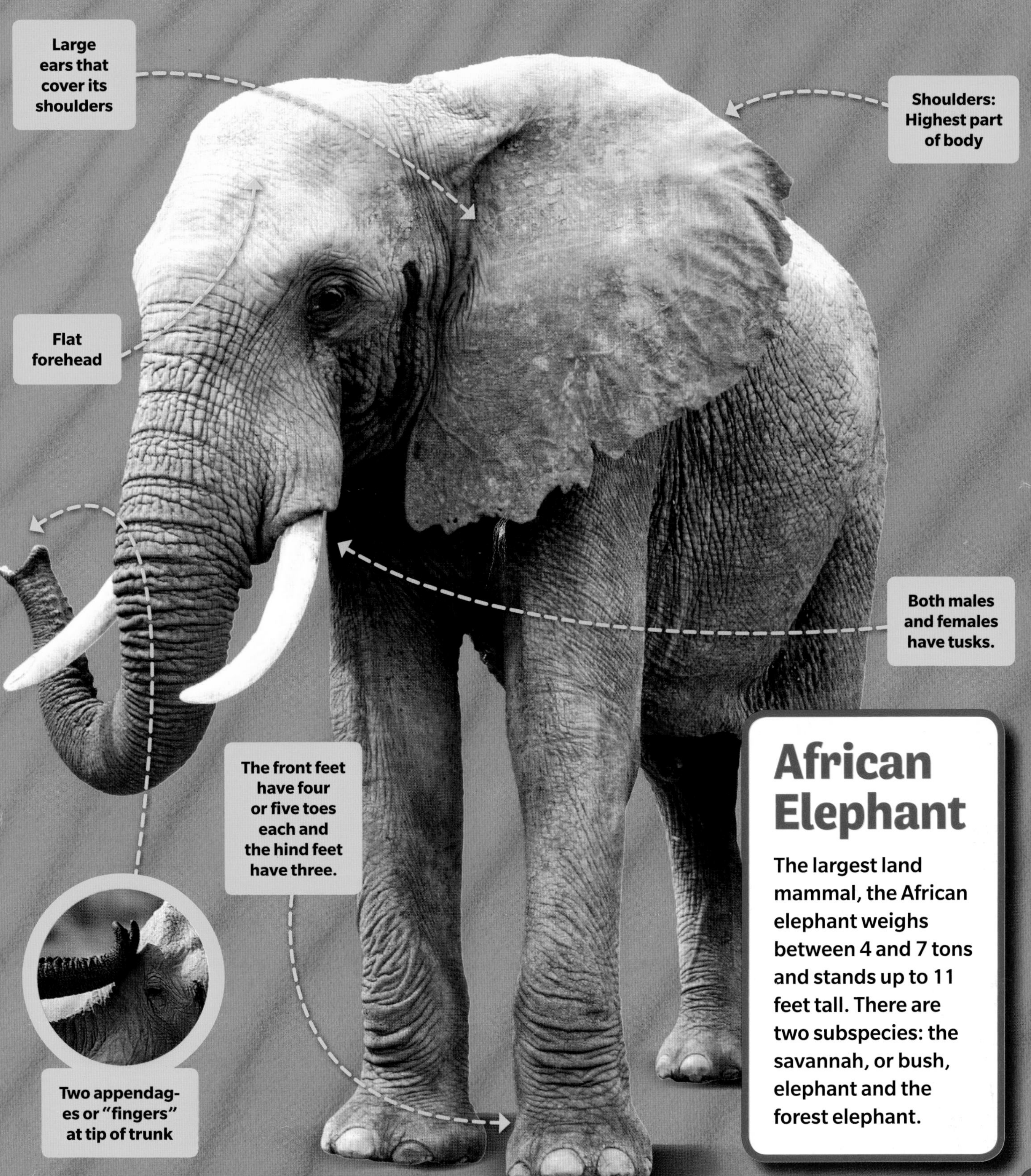

African Elephant

The largest land mammal, the African elephant weighs between 4 and 7 tons and stands up to 11 feet tall. There are two subspecies: the savannah, or bush, elephant and the forest elephant.

Where do animals live in Antarctica?

Seal lovers have given Antarctica the seal of approval because six species of seals live in the waters and on the ice around the frozen continent. The fiercest are leopard seals, which eat seafood but sometimes prefer to eat penguins and other seals. The biggest seals are bull southern elephant seals, which can grow up to 20 feet long. When challenging other males, the bulls inflate their large noses to make their bellows louder and scarier. Elephant seals are champion divers, going almost 5,000 feet deep and staying under for as long as two hours.

Many whales make their summer home in the waters of the Southern Ocean. Blue whales are not only the largest of the baleen whales but also the largest animals on Earth. How big are they? Adults are nearly 100 feet long and their hearts are as big as cars! Among Antarctica's other whales are orcas, the top marine predators also known as killer whales.

◂ Thrills and Krills

Antarctic krill are about the size of your little finger, but their importance is far greater than their size. Millions of these shrimplike sea creatures live in swarms that can spread out for miles and weigh up to two million tons. So what's the big deal? Krill are the main food source of baleen whales and many seals, penguins, fish, and squid.

Fine-Feathered Friends ▸

The most common Antarctic seabirds are penguins. Two of the six Antarctic species—Adélie and emperor penguins—raise their chicks on coastal or sea ice around the continent. The emperor penguin is the largest of the penguins and the only one to breed during Antarctica's frigid winters.

◂ What's Not to Lichen?

Antarctica has no trees or bushes, but it does have about 450 species of plants. Two are flowering plants that grow on the Antarctic Peninsula. The rest are mainly mosses and lichens (lie-kenz). There's life even in the harsh climate of the dry valleys, where scientists have found algae growing inside rocks.

It's Not Big, But It's Hardy ▸

At a quarter of an inch long, the wingless midge (a type of fly) is the largest land animal in Antarctica. Larvae can live without oxygen for up to four weeks and survive even if their body fluids freeze.

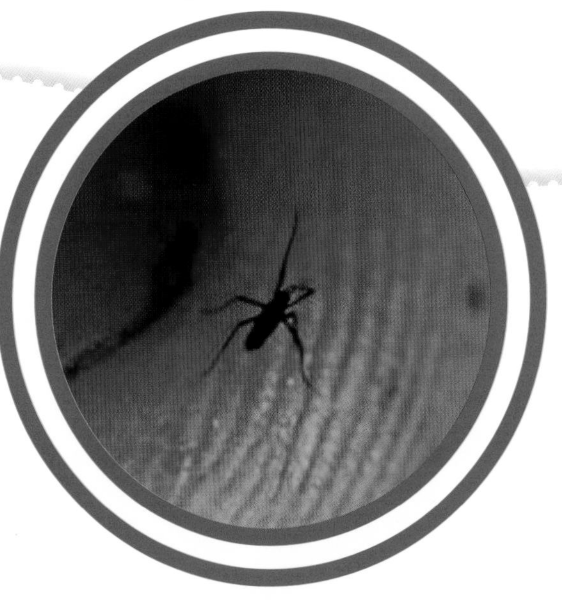

What is an aye-aye?

With big yellow eyes set in a pointy face, large rounded ears, shaggy fur, and an extra-long middle finger that rivals E.T.'s, the aye-aye is one strange-looking creature. But what exactly is it?

Early naturalists believed the aye-aye (eye-eye) to be some type of rodent, possibly a squirrel, because its teeth never stopped growing. Modern scientists say the aye-aye is a primate, a close relative of the lemur. The rare and endangered aye-ayes live in the rainforests of Madagascar, an island off the southeastern coast of Africa.

What Long Fingers You Have!

An aye-aye's bony middle finger is long for a reason. It feeds on tiny insects called grubs, which live deep inside the wood of trees. To reach these tasty morsels, an aye-aye will first tap on dead wood. When the animal's sensitive ears pick up a hollow sound, it begins to gnaw the wood with its sharp teeth. Then it sticks its middle finger deep inside the hole, using its hooked claw to retrieve its meal.

Oh, Baby

Females give birth to one offspring at a time. The young aye-aye stays with its mother until it is around two years old, when it leaves to find its own home.

Why do giraffes have long necks?

Giraffes are the tallest mammals on the planet. Some stand up to 19 feet (5.79 m) high. Some scientists think giraffes have long necks to reach leaves high on trees, especially during periods of drought. Others say giraffes have long necks to help them fight. Male giraffes use their necks as weapons, clubbing their opponents with their heavy skulls.

• Caudipteryx was a feathered peacock-size dinosaur.

When did birds first fly?

Some early birds were actually dinosaurs. Researchers say that millions of years ago, the dinosaur family split. One branch, which included Triceratops and Stegosaurus, kept its feet firmly on the ground. The other branch took flight, giving rise to modern birds.

This tiny hummingbird is descended from huge dinosaurs.

This dinosaur fossil shows an imprint of feathers.

The Birds of Liaoning

Scientists suspected that modern birds evolved from dinosaurs. In 1996, that speculation turned to fact. While tilling his orchard in northwest China, Li Yingfang pulled a slab of rock out of the soil. Inside he found the fossil of a strange creature with the skull of a bird. Imprints in the rock suggested the animal had feathers. Scientists named Li's discovery Sinosauropteryx, which means "Chinese lizard wing." It lived around 125 million years ago.

Birds of a Feather

Before Sinosauropteryx, people believed animals developed feathers for flight. Sinosauropteryx didn't fly. It used its feathers to attract a mate or to defend itself against an attacker. Since Li's discovery, scientists have found other fossils that prove that modern birds evolved from prehistoric dinosaurs, including a distant cousin of the most terrifying predator to walk the planet—Tyrannosaurus rex.

How do honeybees make hives?

You can figure out what this type of insect does by its name. Honeybees make delicious honey, which both bees and humans eat. The flying insects produce honey in a hive that houses up to 60,000 bees. That's like a small city!

When a queen bee decides to build a new hive, scout bees may travel miles to find a tree hollow or other good spot. The scouts lead a swarm of bees to this new location. Honey from the old hive is used to start the new one. Bees chew on honey to turn it into beeswax. The wax is shaped into thousands of six-sided cells. A few layers of cells are called a honeycomb. Workers build combs starting at the top of the hive and work downward. They stick the combs to the roof and walls, making sure there are passageways between the combs. Eventually, bees fill the combs with honey, which feeds them through winter. Sweet!

DID YOU KNOW? TO MAKE A POUND OF HONEY, HONEYBEES LAND ON ABOUT 2 MILLION FLOWERS. THE TOTAL DISTANCE THEY TRAVEL IS ABOUT EQUAL TO CIRCLING THE EARTH TWICE.

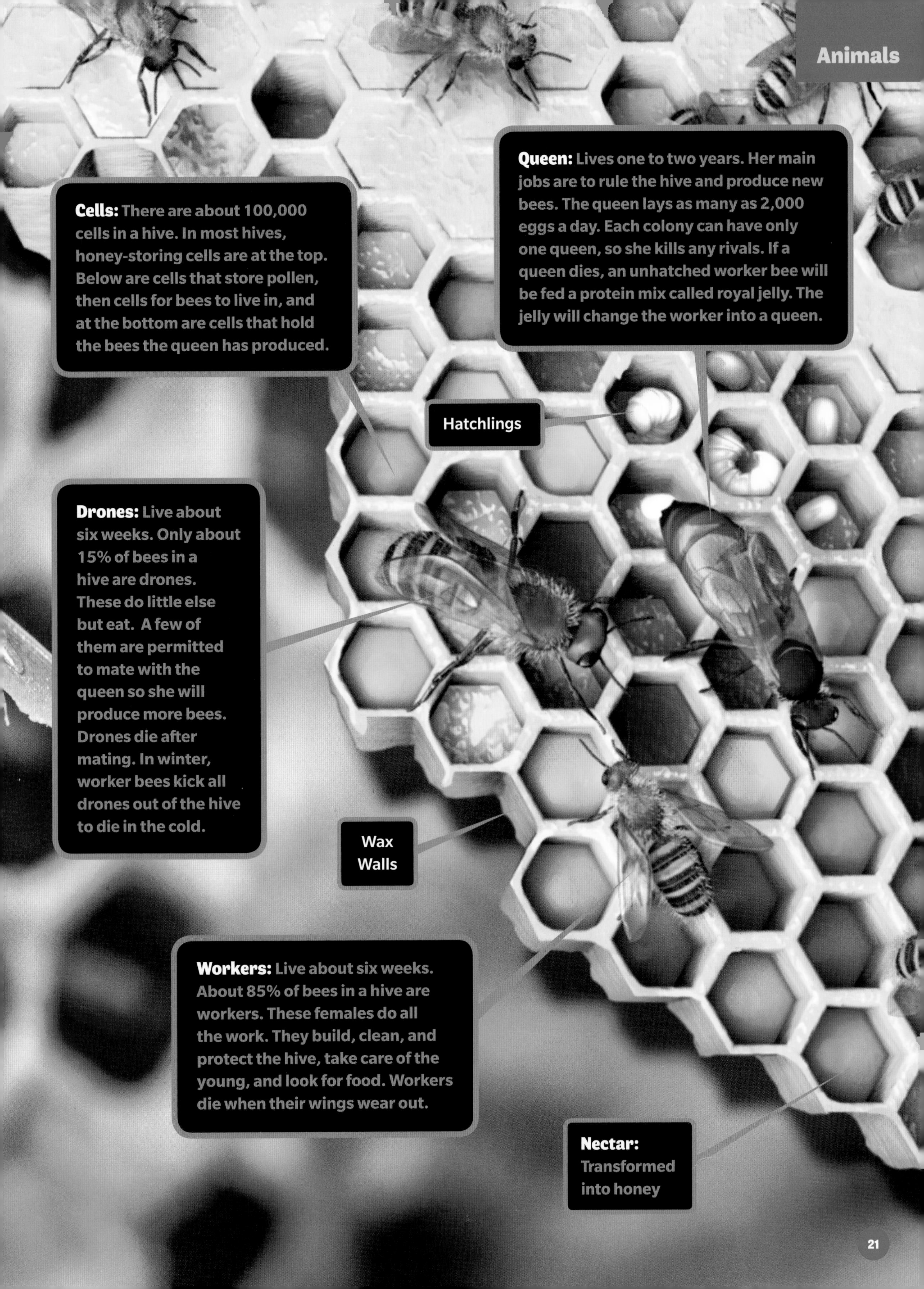

Cells: There are about 100,000 cells in a hive. In most hives, honey-storing cells are at the top. Below are cells that store pollen, then cells for bees to live in, and at the bottom are cells that hold the bees the queen has produced.

Queen: Lives one to two years. Her main jobs are to rule the hive and produce new bees. The queen lays as many as 2,000 eggs a day. Each colony can have only one queen, so she kills any rivals. If a queen dies, an unhatched worker bee will be fed a protein mix called royal jelly. The jelly will change the worker into a queen.

Hatchlings

Drones: Live about six weeks. Only about 15% of bees in a hive are drones. These do little else but eat. A few of them are permitted to mate with the queen so she will produce more bees. Drones die after mating. In winter, worker bees kick all drones out of the hive to die in the cold.

Wax Walls

Workers: Live about six weeks. About 85% of bees in a hive are workers. These females do all the work. They build, clean, and protect the hive, take care of the young, and look for food. Workers die when their wings wear out.

Nectar: Transformed into honey

Why don't cats like water?

Most cats can't swim and don't like the way water feels on their fur. Cats would rather lick their fur to clean it than be bathed in any other way. You can teach some cats to tolerate water if you start training them when they're very young.

Why are so many people afraid of spiders

We're not born afraid of spiders. It's something we learn. Fear of spiders is so common, it has its own name: arachnophobia. Some scientists think humans are naturally worried about animals that move quickly, as spiders do, and the fact that some spiders are poisonous certainly adds to the fear factor.

When did the first zoo open?

In 2009, scientists found an Egyptian animal cemetery that contained the bones of 10 dogs, a baby hippo, and other animals. The site, in the ancient city of Hierakonpolis, is 5,500 years old. Researchers say that the city's rulers kept the animals captive.

The Queen's Menagerie

One of the most famous zoos in ancient history opened in Egypt in 1500 B.C. The zoo was built by Queen Hatshepsut, who collected animals from all over Africa. The oldest zoo in Europe is in Vienna, Austria. It was built by Emperor Franz Josef in 1752, as a gift to his wife.

Philadelphia Zoo

The oldest zoo in the U.S. is the Philadelphia Zoo, in Pennsylvania. It was chartered, or officially registered, in 1859. When it actually opened, in 1874, 3,000 people visited. Admission cost 25 cents for adults and 10 cents for children. The zoo had its own dock so people traveling by steamboat on the Schuylkill River could visit. During its first year, 228,000 people visited the Philadelphia Zoo to see its 813 animals. Today, the zoo is home to 1,300 animals.

● Queen Hatshepsut's zoo included baboons that had been captured in what is now Somalia.

Space

What was the space shuttle?

Thirty years ago, space travel was far from routine. Back then, only a handful of Americans had traveled to space, and they had done so on spacecraft that could only be used once. At the end of the voyage, the crafts would parachute into the ocean, never to be flown again.

All of that changed when NASA rolled out its first space shuttle in 1981. The new spacecraft was designed to blast off using rocket boosters, orbit the Earth, and land like a plane—over and over again.

Shuttle Highs and Lows

In the last 30 years, NASA's five shuttles have completed more than 130 missions. They have helped the agency achieve many goals, from launching flying telescopes to helping to build the International Space Station (ISS), a floating space lab in the sky. The program has also seen its share of darker days. Fourteen lives were tragically lost in two shuttle accidents. After each disaster, NASA paused the shuttle program.

Shuttle History

Here are some of the most important events in the shuttle's past

April 12, 1981
The first shuttle craft, *Columbia*, lifts off, carrying two astronauts.

June 18, 1983
Challenger sails into orbit with Sally Ride. She is the first U.S. woman in space. Two months later, Guion Bluford becomes the first African American to travel into space.

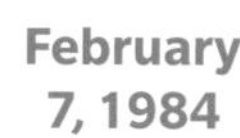

February 7, 1984
An untethered astronaut spacewalks for the first time.

January 28, 1986
Seven crew members lose their lives when *Challenger* explodes shortly after liftoff. NASA suspends flights for nearly three years.

July 21, 2011
Atlantis completes its final mission. NASA retires its shuttle program.

February 1, 2003
Seven astronauts lose their lives as *Columbia* returns to Earth. The shuttle breaks apart minutes before it is expected to land. NASA suspends flights for more than two years.

December 6, 1998
Endeavour delivers the first U.S. piece of the International Space Station.

October 29, 1998
John Glenn, who in 1962 became the first American to orbit Earth, returns to space aboard *Discovery*. At 77, he is the oldest space traveler.

December 2, 1993
Endeavour takes a crew to repair Hubble's mirror. After days of work, Hubble is fixed.

April 24, 1990
Discovery launches the Hubble Space Telescope. Scientists soon realize that there is a defect in Hubble's main mirror, causing pictures to come out blurry.

The End of an Era

On July 21, 2011, the space shuttle *Atlantis* concluded its final mission, marking the end of the space shuttle program. The U.S. government says the space vehicles are too old and too costly to operate. Instead of soaring into space, the shuttles will be on display in museums. And NASA astronauts will be left without a ride of their own. For now, to reach the ISS, they will have to pay to travel aboard Russian spacecraft. Due to recent budget cuts in the space program, American astronauts could be hitchhiking to space for some time.

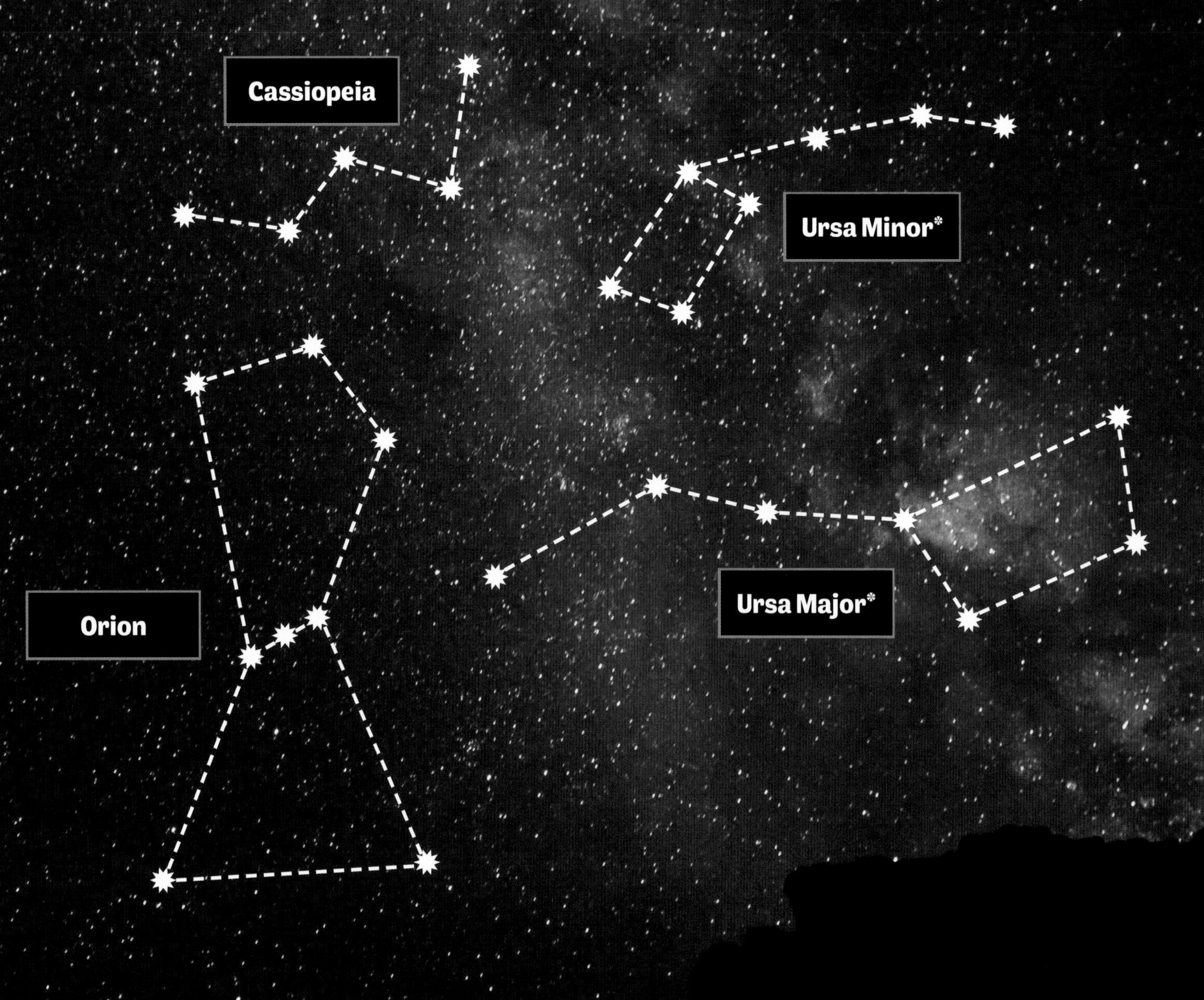

Editor's note: Constellation positions not in relation to one another.

*Shows only part of the constellation.

Why are constellations named as they are?

The ancient Greeks, Babylonians, and Egyptians were among the most avid stargazers. Each civilization named the 88 constellations, or group of stars, for mythological beings. To these ancient people, some of the constellations resembled animals, people, or objects.

Why are there still footprints on Earth's moon?

All the astronauts, rovers, and spacecraft that have visited the moon leave a permanent mark. The moon doesn't have any air or atmosphere, so there's no wind or rain to wipe them away. All previous prints are presumably still visible in the lunar dust.

Where is *Curiosity*?

The Gale Crater on Mars

Curiosity, a robotic vehicle, or "rover," the size of a small SUV, landed on Mars at 1:25 a.m. on August 6, 2012. Two smaller rovers, *Spirit* and *Opportunity*, had landed on the Red Planet in 2004. The newest and biggest Mars rover touched down in the 96-mile-wide Gale Crater in the planet's southern hemisphere.

Curiosity is exploring the crater and climbing the high mountain in its center. It also snaps high-resolution pictures with its 17 cameras, and take rock samples to analyze onboard. NASA scientists are hoping to discover whether life ever existed on Mars.

Curiosity is looking for organics, the carbon-based molecules that are necessary for life to exist. Scientists think they might be found inside rocks. The Gale Crater is a good spot to look because it dates back to about 3.8 billion years ago, when the planet was still covered with water—another requirement for life. *Curiosity* drilled into a rock and tested the powder left by the drill. It showed that life could have existed on Mars—but not whether it actually did.

Why do astronauts exercise in space?

Though we don't always realize it, Earth's gravity pulls on us at all times. We need to exert energy just to move—just walking a few steps is in some ways a workout. But in space, with very little gravity, astronauts must make a special effort to stay healthy. They typically exercise for at least two hours per day.

What is the difference between a comet and an asteroid?

Both comets and asteroids are relatively small objects that orbit the sun and were formed in the early days of our solar system. But there the likeness ends. Comets, often called dirty snowballs, are made up primarily of ice with dust and rock particles mixed in. When comets draw closer to the sun, they begin to vaporize, and a halo, called a coma, forms around them. High-speed solar winds produce the long tails that give comets their distinctive look.

Asteroids come in all shapes and sizes and are composed of rock and metal, leftover scraps from when the solar system formed. Most asteroids orbit in the asteroid belt between Mars and Jupiter.

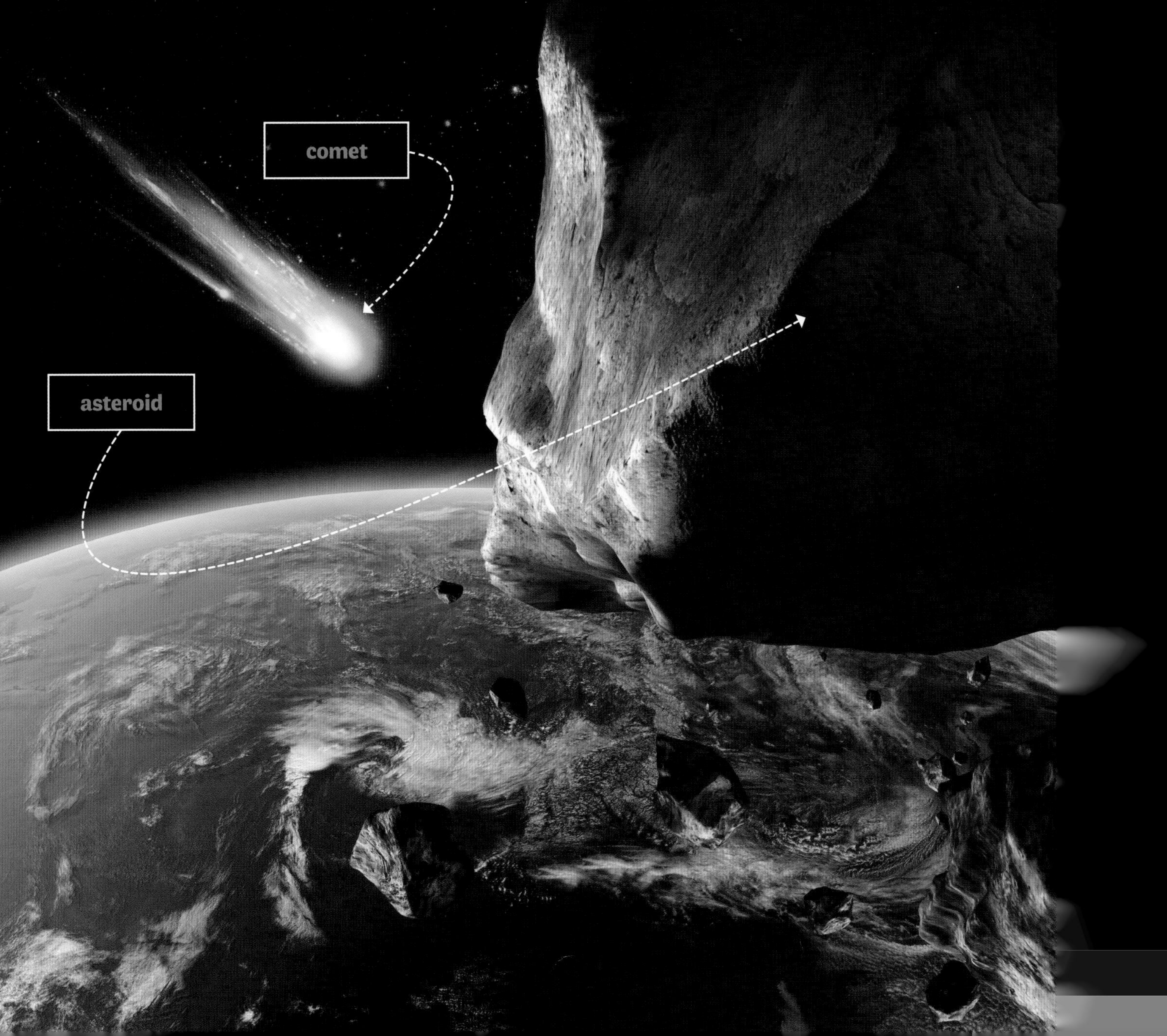

How will the *Juno* probe uncover Jupiter's secrets?

NASA scientists put together the *Juno* spacecraft. They hope it will help reveal the history of Jupiter and the solar system.

Jupiter is the largest planet in the solar system, and it holds some big secrets. Scientists don't know for sure what's going on under the gas giant's 621-mile-thick atmosphere. That may change in 2016, when the unmanned *Juno* spacecraft is scheduled to reach Jupiter after traveling five years. *Juno* will come within 3,000 miles of Jupiter's cloud tops—which, in space terms, is very close. Over one year, *Juno* will send back information during 32 orbits of the planet, including the first clear pictures of the planet's poles.

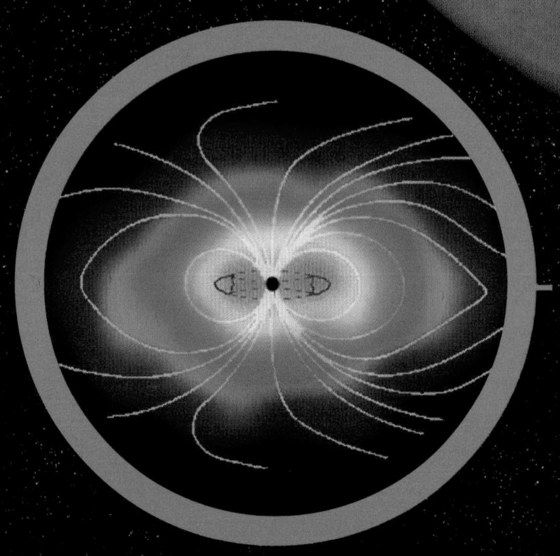

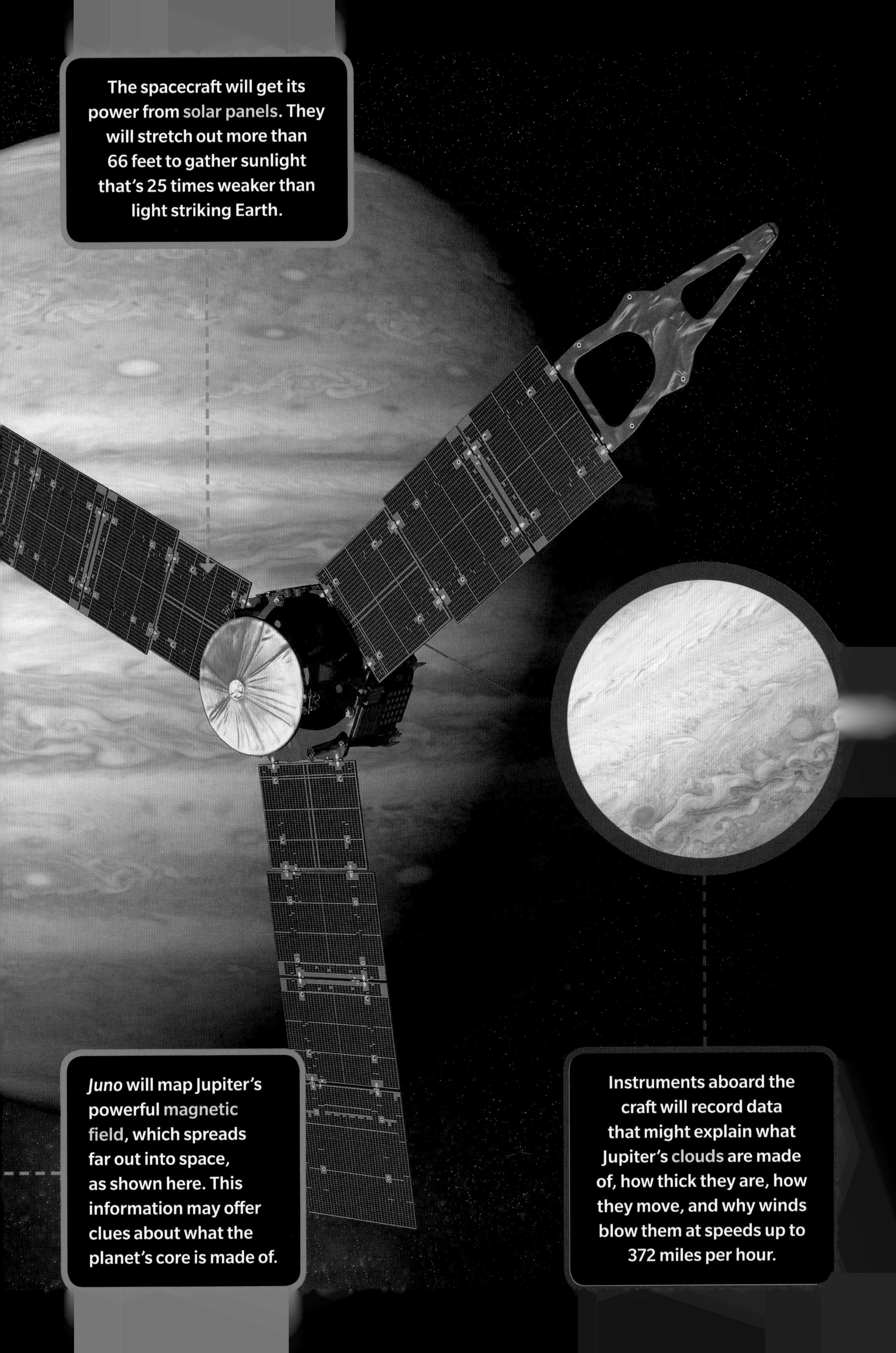

The spacecraft will get its power from solar panels. They will stretch out more than 66 feet to gather sunlight that's 25 times weaker than light striking Earth.

Juno will map Jupiter's powerful magnetic field, which spreads far out into space, as shown here. This information may offer clues about what the planet's core is made of.

Instruments aboard the craft will record data that might explain what Jupiter's clouds are made of, how thick they are, how they move, and why winds blow them at speeds up to 372 miles per hour.

How do astronauts train?

Since the early days of space exploration, astronauts have landed on the moon, walked in space, performed experiments on the space shuttle, and spent time on the International Space Station. Here's a look at some of the training astronauts get at the Lyndon B. Johnson Space Center, in Houston, Texas. Some of these astronauts may one day return to the moon—or blast off for Mars.

Astronauts train for hours in a huge tank of water, which gives the feel of weightlessness. They do tasks in the water that they will do in zero gravity during space flight. One tank, the Neutral Buoyancy Laboratory, is 200 feet long and 40 feet deep. It's the largest indoor pool in the world.

To experience weightlessness, astronauts ride on airplanes that go high up and then dive. For 30 seconds during each dive, astronauts float around the cabin in zero-gravity conditions.

Astronauts practice living and working in mockups—copies of the spacecraft they'll fly. They also train in simulators that reproduce the events of a mission. Trainers give the crew problems to solve or put them in emergency situations.

Astronauts-in-training learn aircraft safety, including how to eject and parachute from a plane. They also take flight training. Space pilots have learned to fly aircraft built to work like the space shuttle.

Candidates receive survival training. They are taught how to stay alive if their craft lands in the ocean or in a forest. They experience tough challenges so they know what to do in a real situation.

The people on the ground who give information to astronauts during missions are called the flight-control team. An astronaut crew practices an upcoming mission with a particular flight-control team.

Why do we call Mars the Red Planet?

We should really call Mars the Rusty Planet. Its soil is rich in iron oxides, known to Earthlings as rust. Iron oxides are chemical compounds made up of iron and oxygen that give off a reddish color. Some ancient people used to think that blood caused the reddish glow of Mars.

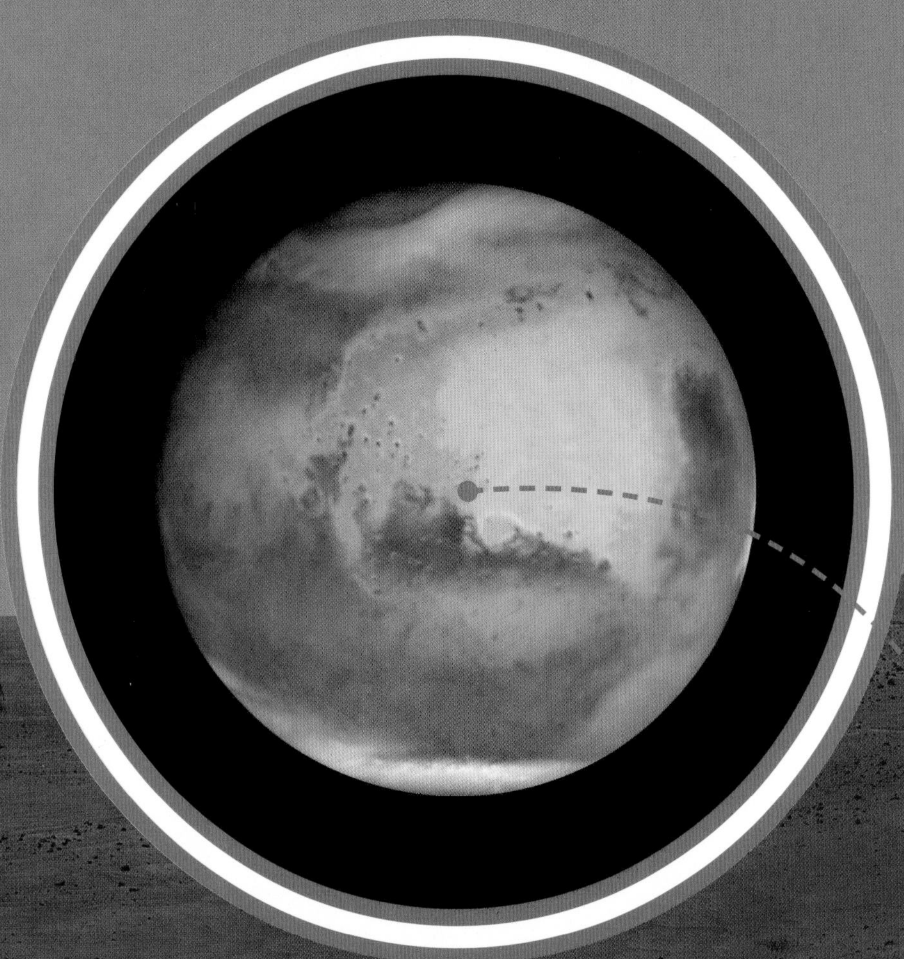

● The soil on Mars is rich with iron oxides, also known as rust.

DID YOU KNOW? THE ATMOSPHERE ON MARS IS MADE UP MOSTLY OF CARBON DIOXIDE, A GAS WHICH TREES ON EARTH LOVE BUT IS POISONOUS TO HUMANS.

How do rockets reach space?

The gravity of the Earth is very strong and pulls everything toward its surface. It takes a lot of energy to overcome that pull. Rockets are mostly filled with fuel that burns fast, pushing the rocket beyond our atmosphere. Once they reach space, they need far less fuel to fly.

People and Places

Where is the Lost City of the Inca?

In 1911, an 11-year-old Peruvian boy led American archaeologist Hiram Bingham to some ruins high on a ridge overlooking the Urubamba River in southeast Peru. When Bingham saw walls and terraces among the overgrowth, he was sure he'd discovered Vilcabamba, the fabled Lost City of the Inca. Bingham held on to this belief until his death in 1957. In fact, he had found the ruins of a lost Inca city—just not the one he'd been looking for.

The city Bingham found was Machu Picchu, a masterpiece of Inca engineering. The remains of buildings and plazas stand on more than 700 walled terraces that were built to provide level areas. Beneath the terraces, a drainage system of crushed rock helps keep the city from slipping down the steep mountainside during the heavy rains between December and March. A water system channels spring water to fountains and baths.

Machu Picchu has stood for more than 500 years—even though no mortar was used in any of the walls. Instead, the stones were shaped and fit together so perfectly that even a knife blade can't slip between them. The walls, including doors and windows, tilt inward from bottom to top. When an earthquake hits, the stones "dance" around and then settle back into place.

DID YOU KNOW? MACHU PICCHU WAS PROBABLY BUILT FOR AN INCAN KING. AT ITS MOST POWERFUL, THE EMPIRE STRETCHED NORTH FROM THE CAPITAL OF CUSCO, PERU, INTO PARTS OF WHAT ARE NOW THE NATIONS OF ECUADOR, COLOMBIA, BOLIVIA, ARGENTINA, AND CHILE. THE EMPIRE WAS CONNECTED BY MORE THAN 14,000 MILES OF ROADS—SOME OF WHICH STILL EXIST.

Why is the Sphinx a symbol of Egypt?

The Sphinx, a lion with a human head, was believed to have divine power. Ancient Egyptians built many Sphinx statues. This one, Egypt's Great Sphinx of Giza, is the world's largest, measuring 66 feet (20 m) high and 241 feet (73 m) long. Many historians believe the roughly 4,500-year-old big cat was built to guard the Great Pyramids that stand right behind it. The sandstone monument was buried under sand for many centuries. Over time, water and pollution have chipped away at its surface.

Where was the Silk Road?

The Silk Road wasn't just one road but a number of trade routes that stretched across Asia from the Mediterranean Sea to Chang'an (now Xian) in eastern China, with branches to India. Camel caravans going east carried wool, gold, glass, and other goods from Europe and Africa. In China and India, the merchants traded their goods for silks, jade, spices, and other things to sell at home. Along the way, cities became centers where people also traded ideas, customs, beliefs, music, and artistic styles.

Across central Asia, the Silk Road wound thousands of miles over harsh deserts and high mountains Between cities, travelers stopped at oases to rest. After the tenth century, they could stay at caravansaries (care-uh-*van*-suh-reez). These large stone buildings served as inns, where people and their animals could rest and be safe from bandits.

When did the ancient Romans rule the world?

Rome was the world's largest and longest-lasting empire. The ancient Roman Empire existed from 27 B.C. to 476 A.D. By 50 B.C., the empire stretched across Europe, Northern Africa, and parts of the Middle East. By 200 A.D., wars with northern "barbarians" weakened the empire, which completely collapsed in 476 A.D.

Early Republic

Before Rome was a great empire, it was a small city on the Italian peninsula. In 509 B.C., the Romans established a republic where there were no kings or queens. The Roman Senate made laws and controlled the government.

The End

Although historians say many factors led to Rome's demise, the beginning of the end was in 376–382 A.D., when the Romans fought a series of battles with the Goths, who invaded Rome from the north. By 476 A.D., the once-mighty empire was crushed.

● The Roman Colosseum still draws visitors today.

Powerful Army

The Romans ruled a vast area for hundreds of years. Their army had about 350,000 men. Roman soldiers were so good that no one beat them in battle for 500 years. The Romans also ruled through fear and intimidation. In 73–71 B.C., an ex-gladiator named Spartacus led a slave revolt. The Romans captured the rebels and later executed them.

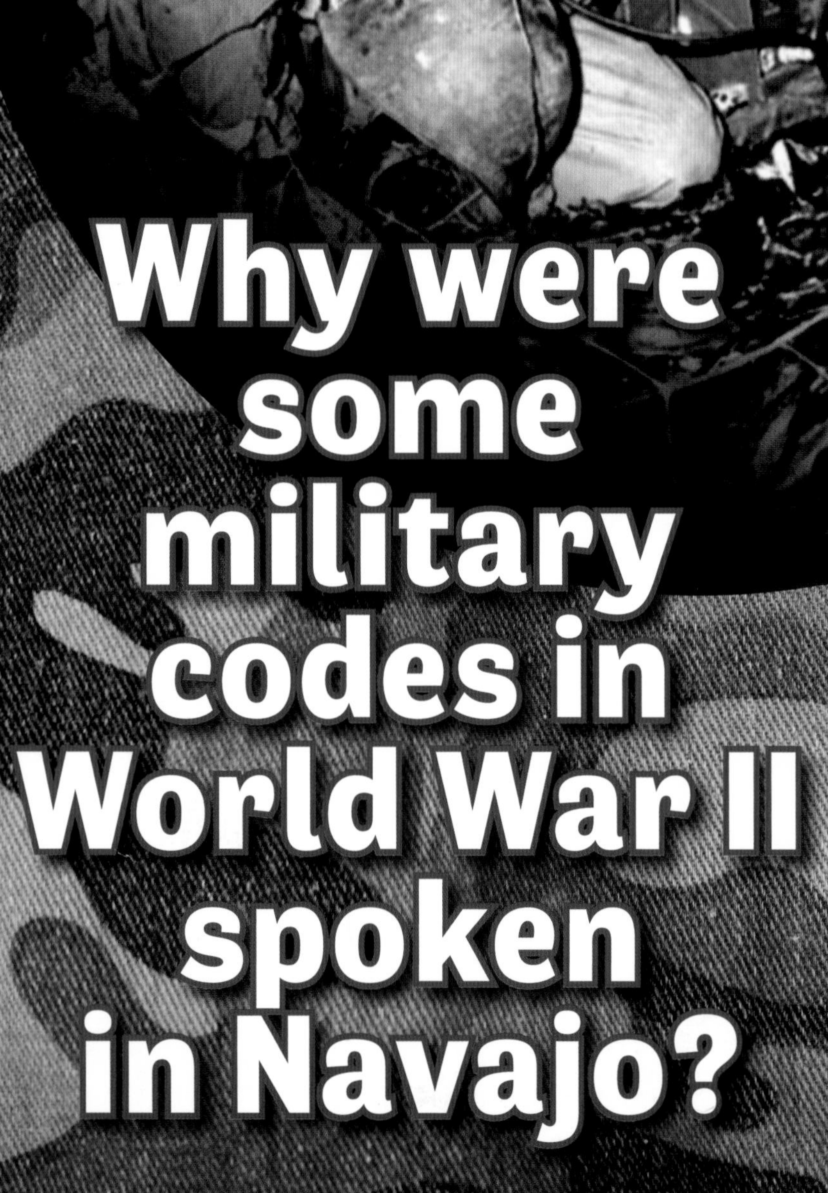

Why were some military codes in World War II spoken in Navajo?

The Japanese were experts at breaking secret U.S. military codes used for sending messages. A Marine named Philip Johnston, who knew how to speak Navajo, had an idea to use the Navajo language to send messages. Only a few people outside the Navajo nation knew the language. The Navajos who sent and translated messages were called code talkers.

Where did scientists find the oldest human ancestors?

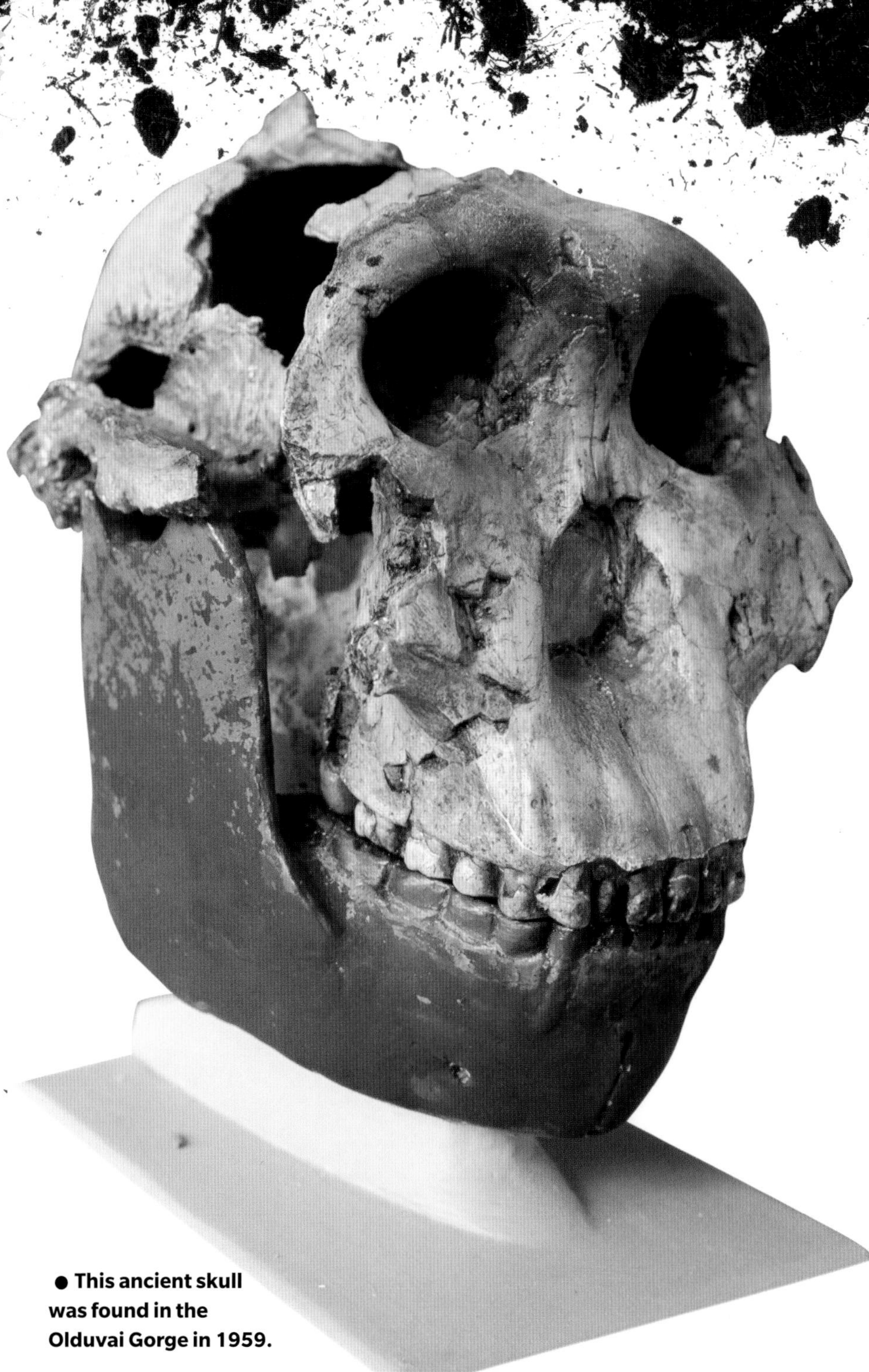

● This ancient skull was found in the Olduvai Gorge in 1959.

Many of the bones and other fossil remains of ancient human ancestors were discovered at dig sites in the Great Rift Valley in Ethiopia and Tanzania. It makes sense when you think about it. If man and apes share common ancestors, the natural place to look for their fossil remains would be in Africa, where most of the great apes come from.

Tanzania's Olduvai Gorge is the most famous of the Rift Valley dig sites. After more than 20 years of digging, scientists Louis and Mary Leakey made their first discovery. In 1959, they found a skull that belonged to a stage between apes and people. It was .25–1.75 million years old. Since then, other discoveries have been made in the Rift Valley, including the remains of a 4.2 million-year-old species identified in 1994 by Meave Leakey, Louis and Mary Leakey's daughter-in-law.

Why did Dr. Martin Luther King Jr. give his "I Have a Dream" speech?

On August 28, 1963, Martin Luther King Jr. spoke before a crowd of 250,000 people in Washington, D.C. The historic event, called the March on Washington, was a rally calling for civil rights, jobs, and general equality for African Americans. The march ended at the Lincoln Memorial, where Dr. King gave one of the greatest speeches in U.S. history. The powerful energy of the event strongly influenced lawmakers to pass the 1964 Civil Rights Act and the 1965 Voting Rights Act.

Why did the Maya build pyramids?

Deep within the jungles of Mexico and Central America, the Maya, a Native American civilization, built amazing pyramids. The Maya began building pyramids mostly for religious purposes some 3,000 years ago. Some pyramids had stairs so people could climb to the top and hold sacrificial rituals. The Maya built the pyramids taller than the surrounding jungle so people could use them as landmarks. The Maya also used some pyramids as tombs for important government officials.

How was Mount Rushmore built?

The four heads carved on Mount Rushmore, located in the Black Hills of South Dakota, are big shots in every way. The heads of Presidents George Washington, Thomas Jefferson, Theodore Roosevelt, and Abraham Lincoln are each 60 feet tall. Their features are huge: Each nose is 20 feet long, the mouths are 18 feet wide, and each eye is 11 feet across. If their bodies were built to scale, they would be 46 stories high.

During the summer, more than 20,000 visitors come each day to admire the humongous monument. Sculptor Gutzon Borglum began the project in 1927, and it was completed in 1941. During that time, 450,000 tons of granite, a type of stone, was removed from Mount Rushmore, mostly by dynamite. Those explosives helped create one of the largest works of art in the world. ▶

1. Mount Rushmore was picked because the rock could be easily carved. Also, the mountainside received a lot of sunlight, so visitors could view it for most of the day.

2. Borglum made a small model of the four presidents. Each inch on the model represented one foot on the mountain. Workers used the model to create the sculpture on the mountain.

3. A worker prepares dynamite charges. The dynamite removed rock to within three or four inches of the finished faces, creating the shape of lips, cheeks, noses, necks, and brows.

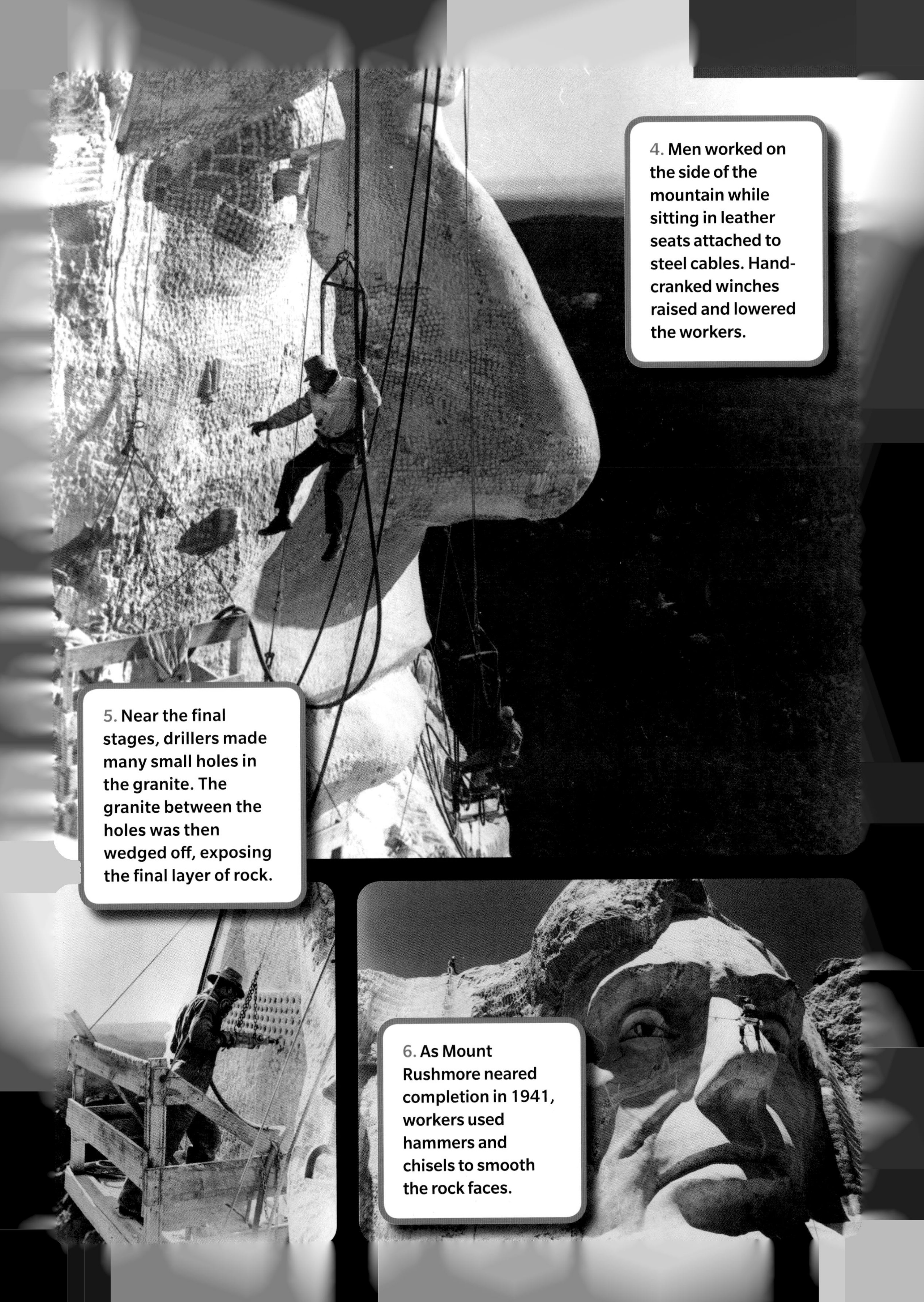

4. Men worked on the side of the mountain while sitting in leather seats attached to steel cables. Hand-cranked winches raised and lowered the workers.

5. Near the final stages, drillers made many small holes in the granite. The granite between the holes was then wedged off, exposing the final layer of rock.

6. As Mount Rushmore neared completion in 1941, workers used hammers and chisels to smooth the rock faces.

Why was Genghis Khan called the Universal Ruler?

Genghis Khan came from Mongolia, which is now in Northern China. Around 1175 A.D., at the age of 20, the warrior gathered a great army that conquered and united most of Asia. Because he was the leader of their leaders, his subjects called him Universal Ruler. At the time, Khan's Mongol empire became the largest empire the world had ever seen.

Where was the first capital of the United States?

It was summer 1788. Eleven out of 13 states had ratified the Constitution. Now it was time to put it into operation. But where should the capital of the young United States be located? Some members of the Congress argued for Philadelphia or Lancaster, Pennsylvania, or for Annapolis or Baltimore, Maryland. Other members fought for the new seat of government to be in the same place where they were already meeting. They won the argument, and New York City became the first capital.

The first Federal Congress met at the newly remodeled Federal Hall on Wall Street on March 4, 1789. However, the weather was bad and not enough senators and representatives had arrived to conduct business. It was another month before everyone could gather and count the electoral votes for the nation's first president. With 69 out of 138 votes, George Washington became the country's leader. John Adams, with the second-highest number of votes, became vice president.

On April 30, 1789, Washington took the oath of office on the balcony of Federal Hall. Eliza Quincy, an eyewitness, wrote that "the windows and the roofs of the houses were crowded, and in the streets the throng was so dense that it seemed as if one might literally walk on the heads of the people." After Washington was sworn in, a 13-cannon salute was fired and "All the bells in the city rang out a peal of joy."

● This print shows George Washington taking the oath of office at New York City's Federal Hall.

Science

How do wind turbines make electricity?

Wind can sometimes be a destructive force. But wind is also a great help to humans. Over the centuries, windmills have been used to pump water, drain lakes, cut wood, and grind grain. Today, a kind of windmill is being used to produce electricity. Called wind turbines, these machines make in one year only a little over one percent of the total electricity generated in the U.S. Still, this is enough to power the entire state of Colorado.

The amount of electricity generated by wind has been growing over the last few years. One big reason is that wind is renewable energy, which means it will never run out. Also, wind turbines don't cause pollution, are cheap to run, and don't take up much space compared to the energy they produce. Some people think the answer to our energy problems is blowing in the wind.

Wind turbines are built tall to catch winds that often blow high above the ground. Most are as tall as a 20-story building, while some are twice that tall.

The **casing** holds the drive shaft, gears, and a generator.

Wind makes the lightweight **blades** turn. The faster the blades spin, the more electricity is produced. The blades are connected to the drive shaft.

The drive shaft turns **gears**, which make another drive shaft spin even faster. This drive shaft leads to a generator.

As the blades turn, the drive shaft spins. The **drive shaft** is connected to the gears.

The **generator** changes the spin of the drive shaft into an electrical current.

Electricity from the generator flows down wires to a **transformer**. This device makes the current stronger. The electricity is sent through power lines to homes and towns.

Why do compasses always point north?

Because the Earth has an iron core, its spinning creates a magnetic field. It's as if a giant magnet were buried in the center of the Earth, with the north and south poles as the tips. The needle of a compass is a small magnet balanced on a single point. Since the magnet in the compass always lines up with the Earth's magnetic field, one end always points north and the other always points south.

DID YOU KNOW? IF THE EARTH WEREN'T TILTED, SOME PARTS OF THE PLANET WOULD ALWAYS BE FROZEN AND OTHERS WOULD ALWAYS BE HOT. ON PLANETS WITH EXTREME TILTS, LIKE URANUS, THE SEASONS LAST FOR YEARS INSTEAD OF MONTHS.

What is GPS?

Before maps or compasses were invented, people used the sun and stars to navigate. In a way, we're still looking to the sky when we travel—only now we're looking to high-tech satellites, called the Global Positioning System (GPS).

GPS is a system of satellites, monitoring stations, and receivers. The 28 solar-powered satellites are spaced evenly around Earth and orbit our planet twice a day. Each satellite carries four atomic clocks that send the exact time to receivers on Earth. Each satellite also sends signals that tell its current location. A GPS receiver uses the information to calculate its own position on Earth.

How do roller coasters go up and down?

A roller coaster is like a scary movie: It gives riders thrills and chills without putting them in danger. How do these scream machines move people up, down, and around? It takes energy. As a roller coaster car is pulled up the first hill, it stores potential energy. The higher it goes, the more potential energy it has. When gravity pulls the coaster down the track, the coaster releases the potential energy. Now it has kinetic energy, which is the energy an object has when it moves. The faster an object moves, the more kinetic energy it has. The coaster is moving fastest after it goes down the first and highest hill. This gives the car enough energy to go up the next hill.

A coaster can't go up and down hills forever. Air resistance and the friction of the wheels against the track make the car lose energy and eventually slow down. That's why each hill is made smaller and smaller.

Motorized chains pull the cars up the first hill. Some rides use magnets in the cars and track to pull the coaster quickly up the first hill.

The **first hill** is the highest. The coaster gains enough kinetic energy going down this hill to go up the next hill. The second hill is next highest. At the bottom of the second one, the car has just enough energy to reach the top of the third hill.

Safety bars and heavy seat belts keep riders inside the car.

Three sets of **car wheels** run above, under, and alongside the track. They keep the car locked on when it makes twists, turns, and loop-de-loops.

Riders on a **loop-de-loop** don't fall out thanks to centrifugal (cen-*trif*-uh-gull) force. The force of the car moving in a circle pushes riders back toward the floor of the car.

How do tornadoes form?

A tornado is a column of rapidly rotating air that generally begins life as a thunderstorm. The atmosphere becomes unstable when warm, moist air bangs into a wall of cool, dry air. A layer of warm, humid air sits near the ground and a layer of cold air is in the upper atmosphere. The warm air rises. The cold air falls. A tornado is born when the wind's speed and direction causes the rising air to rotate vertically in the middle of the storm.

Why does Tornado Alley get more tornadoes than other places?

Tornado Alley is a part of the United States stretching from Texas to North Dakota. Although tornadoes occur throughout the U.S., they take place more often and with more force in Tornado Alley. Why is that? Tornado Alley is flat. It is also where warm, moist air from the Gulf of Mexico and cold, dry air from Canada collide. When that happens, tornadoes are born.

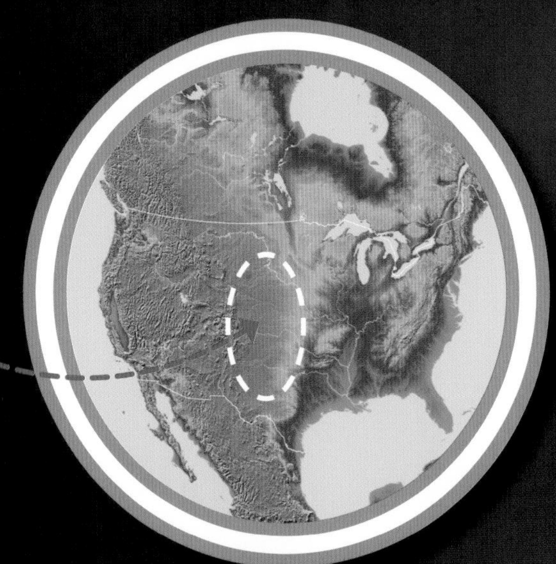

How does the sun stay hot?

The temperature of the sun's surface is about 10,000°F. At its core, the sun is more than 27,000,000°F. The ancient Greeks believed the sun's heat came from a huge lump of coal that burned in its center. In the 1800s, some scientists thought the sun was filled with erupting volcanoes. Others believed the sun got hot from millions of meteorites striking it.

The sun started out as a massive ball of gas and dust. About 4.5 billion years ago, gravity squeezed together the particles so tightly, they produced heat—and the sun was born. But how does it continue to burn? Inside the sun, the intense heat at its birth started a process called nuclear fusion. Nuclear fusion happens when hydrogen atoms in the sun's core combine, or fuse, to form the element helium. This releases energy, which reaches Earth (93 million miles away) mostly in the form of light and heat. The sun has plenty of hydrogen, so it should keep us warm for about 5 billion more years.

Core: The center takes up only two percent of the sun's space, but holds 60 percent of its mass. Here, immense heat and pressure slam together parts of hydrogen atoms. The atoms fuse into helium atoms, releasing almost all the energy that keeps the sun shining.

Radiative Zone: The energy from the core rises in the form of particles called photons (*foh*-tahnz). Here, the energy of the photons is absorbed by various atoms. Those atoms then give off more energy. This way, energy slowly rises to the convective zone.

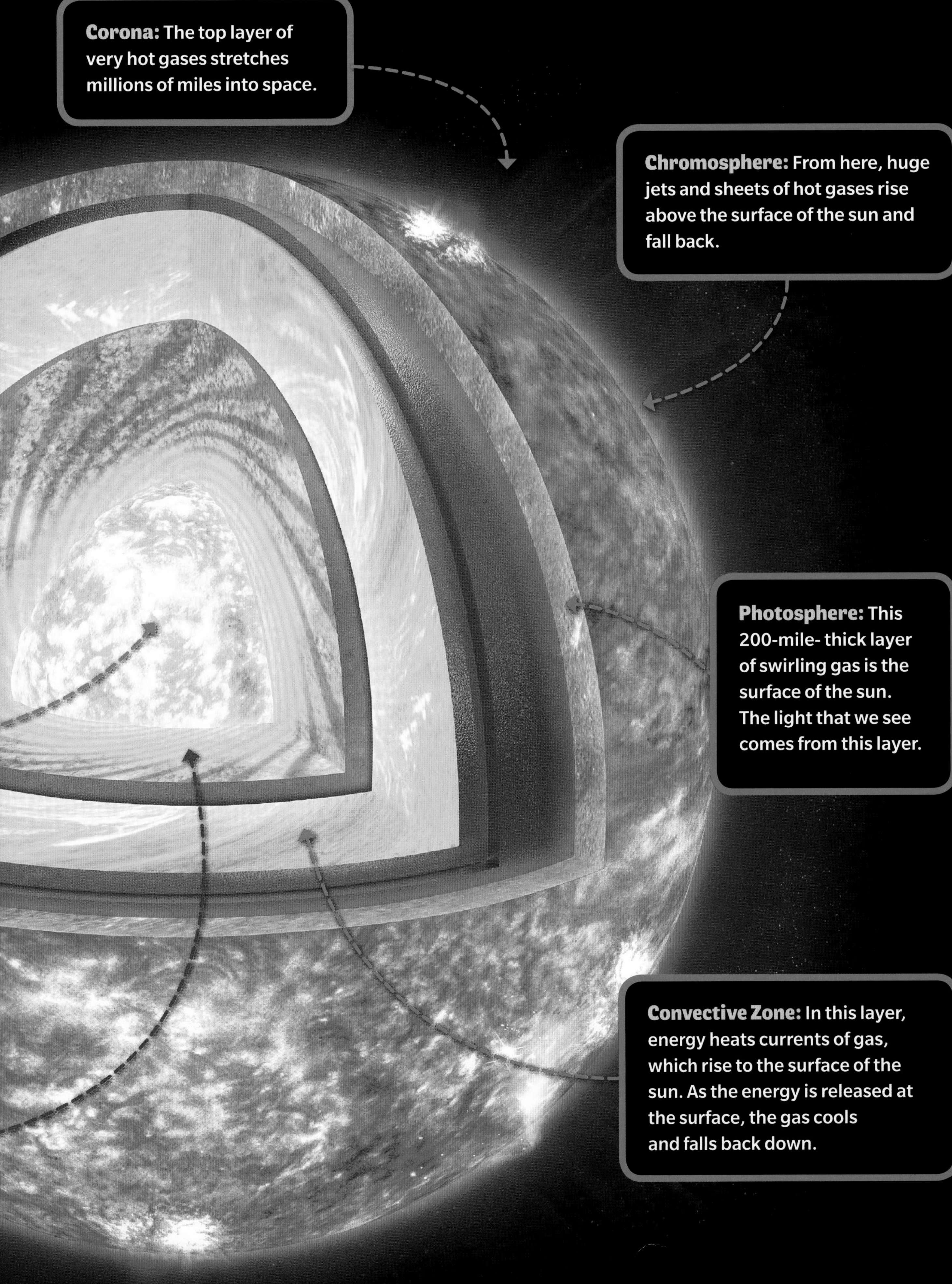
Corona: The top layer of very hot gases stretches millions of miles into space.
Chromosphere: From here, huge jets and sheets of hot gases rise above the surface of the sun and fall back.
Photosphere: This 200-mile- thick layer of swirling gas is the surface of the sun. The light that we see comes from this layer.
Convective Zone: In this layer, energy heats currents of gas, which rise to the surface of the sun. As the energy is released at the surface, the gas cools and falls back down.

Where does your electricity come from?

Flipping a switch may be easy, but it's only the last step in getting electricity to turn on the lights, the TV, the computer, and most appliances in your home. But where does electricity come from and how does it get to the switch?

1. Electricity is produced in power plants. Most of the plants use fuel, such as coal, natural gas, nuclear power, or garbage, to boil water. The steam from the hot water spins large blades in engines called turbines to create energy. Another machine, called a generator, turns the mechanical energy produced by the turbines into electricity. In hydroelectric plants, water is used to turn the turbines. Solar energy, wind power, and geothermal energy—heat created deep inside Earth—can also be used to create electricity.

2. After the electricity has been produced, it goes through transformers that increase the voltage, or intensity. This high-voltage electricity is then sent through long-distance cables to substations. There, it goes through more transformers, this time to lower the voltage.

3. The electricity leaves the substation through power lines. Smaller transformers on utility poles or in boxes lower the voltage even more until the electricity is safe to use in your home.

4. On the way into your house, the electricity runs through a meter that measures how much you use.

5. Next, it goes through a fuse box or circuit breaker that keeps the house safe in case an appliance causes a sudden accidental surge of electricity. From there, it passes through wires in the walls to the switches and electrical outlets.

What is acid rain?

Most people think that rain is pure, clean water. But even clean rain contains some acid, though not enough to cause harm.

Acid rain, however, has way more acid than clean rain. In fact, some drops are almost as acidic as vinegar. Acid rain doesn't even have to be rain. It can be any precipitation, such as snow, sleet, or fog, that has unusually high amounts of acid.

Rain Pollution

Acid rain is caused by air pollution. The coal, oil, and natural gas we burn to run power plants, factories, homes, and vehicles, release gases into the air. Two in particular, sulfur dioxide and nitrogen oxide, are especially dangerous, at least when they combine with water vapor to become sulfuric acid or nitric acid. Acid rain damages the environment, washing away nutrients in soil. It can kill fish and other marine life. Acid rain even harms buildings as it dissolves minerals in stone.

Acid rain killed the spruce trees in this forest.

Why does every living thing have DNA?

● DNA molecules form a double helix.

DID YOU KNOW? EVERY LIVING THING IS MADE MOSTLY OF FOUR BASIC ELEMENTS: HYDROGEN, CARBON, NITROGEN, AND OXYGEN. OF THESE, CARBON IS THE ONLY SOLID ELEMENT. THE REST ARE GASES.

All living things are made up of cells. Complex plants and animals can each have billions or even trillions of cells, each with a specific job to do. DNA is the chemical that carries the structure for every living thing—a kind of code that tells each cell what to do. DNA is made up of genes that contain information that determines how living things act and appear. Each of your tiny cells has about six feet of DNA coiled inside of it.

Sports

How does an arena change an ice rink into a basketball court?

Ice hockey and basketball couldn't be more different. Hockey players bang into each other as they skate on ice. Basketball players run and jump on a wooden floor.

Even though the games and playing surfaces are very different, the sports are often played in the same arena—and on the same day! How do workers make the changeover? Here's how it works in the STAPLES Center, located in Los Angeles, California.

3:49
The Los Angeles Kings beat the Boston Bruins, 4–3. The game went into overtime, so the STAPLES Center workers have less time than usual to get ready for an NBA game, which is set to start in less than four hours.

3:59
The crew first takes down the glass around the rink. Forklifts help remove the glass. Then workers begin to cover the ice with more than 600 panels, which protect the ice surface and help keep it frozen.

4:38
After workers cover the floor with panels, they put down the basketball floor. They start at the center and build outward. The court is made of 217 pieces that are numbered and come out stacked on top of one another.

4:57
The crew cleans dust off the floor with a special solution. The netting around the rink is lifted to the ceiling. The crew also removes the penalty boxes and team benches. For basketball, an extra 80 seats are added.

5:23
TV crews and photographers begin to set up their cameras when the floor is three-quarters complete. The scoreboard, called the JumboTron, is being switched from hockey to basketball graphics.

7:44
The game starts between the Los Angeles Clippers and the Cleveland Cavaliers. The STAPLES Center crew makes this changeover about 200 times a year. These veterans need only a few hours to complete the transformation.

Where was the first FIFA World Cup played?

An aerial view of the stadium in Montevideo, Uruguay, where the final game for the first FIFA World Cup was played.

On July 30, 1930, more than 80,000 people crowded into a brand-new stadium in Montevideo, Uruguay. They were there to watch the home team and Argentina compete for the first FIFA World Cup. Since its founding in 1904, FIFA—Fédération Internationale de Football Association, or the International Soccer Association—had wanted to stage a world championship, and the game was finally at hand.

Planning had begun in 1928. Italy, Netherlands, Spain, Sweden, and Uruguay were interested in hosting. FIFA chose Uruguay, which would celebrate 100 years of independence in 1930—and had offered to build a new stadium as well as pay travel expenses for the teams. Thirteen teams signed up to play, including the U.S., Mexico, seven South American countries, and four European nations.

In the final match, Argentina was ahead 2–1 at halftime. But in the second half, Uruguay scored three more goals to win the first World Cup 4–2.

Why was Earvin Johnson called Magic?

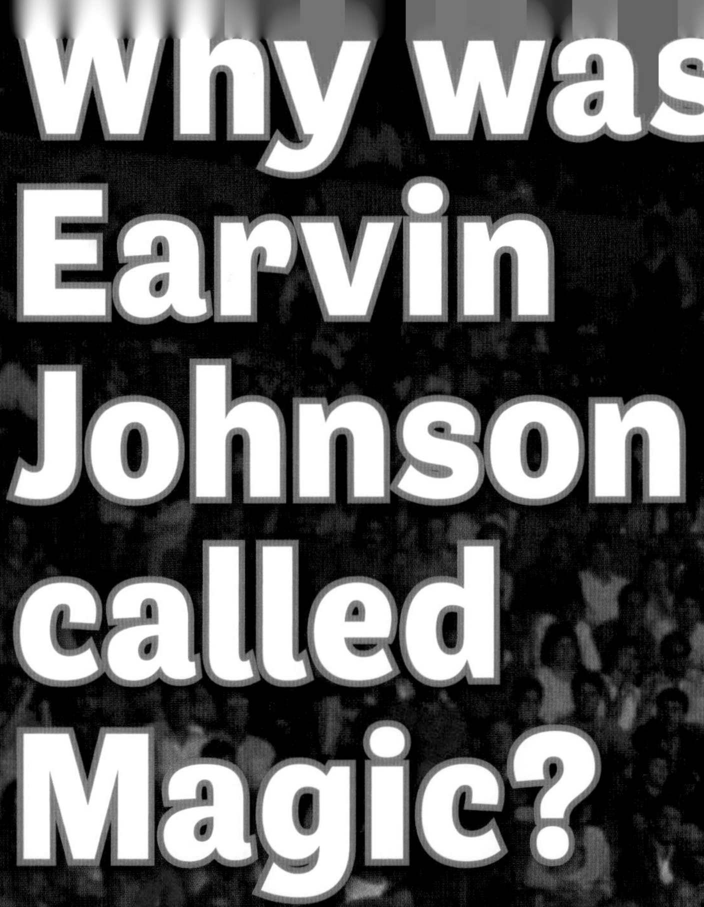

Magic Johnson got his name thanks to his amazing passing ability and his style on the court. A sports writer decided that Magic best described the way Earvin played. Until he came along, players of his size (6-foot-9, 220 pounds) rarely played point guard or passed very often. Johnson brought flair to the NBA, where he played from 1979 to 1991, and again during the 1995–96 season.

What is the world's longest dog sled race?

Dashing through the snow in a 12-dog open sled... It isn't likely that people who take part in the Iditarod, a grueling sled dog race, would have time to sing that version of *Jingle Bells*. They are too busy driving their dog teams over 1,049 miles of snow and ice in Alaska. There are two trails, one used in even-numbered years, the other in odd-numbered years. Both start in Anchorage and both end in Nome. On the first Saturday in March, each driver, called a musher, stands at the rear of the sled behind the hitched pairs of dogs. At the signal, more than 50 mushers and their dog teams start the race.

Mushing to the Finish Line

For the next two weeks, humans and animals will face harsh conditions, including below-freezing temperatures, biting wind, and blizzards. Along the way are checkpoints where the mushers sign in so that officials can be sure they are following the correct route and not taking shortcuts.

After days of cold and ice and snow, the first musher enters Nome driving the sled toward the finish line, which is a wooden arch. A lantern hanging on the arch stays lit until the last musher glides through as thousands of fans cheer.

Why do some race cars have "wings"?

In car racing, the faster a car travels the greater its lift, or tendency to rise. When lift becomes too great, it causes the car to lose its grip on the road, making it hard to control. Race cars have wing-shaped parts called spoilers to fight off this lift. The spoilers create a downward force, which helps keep the car on the road.

Why do hockey goalies wear masks?

Hockey goalies did not always wear face masks. In 1930, Clint Benedict, of the Montreal Maroons, first wore a mask in competition after a puck smashed into his face. He took the mask off after a few games. In 1959, Jacques Plante, the goaltender for the Montreal Canadiens, became the first goalie in NHL history to put on a face mask for good. Plante had been practicing with a fiberglass mask, but Canadiens coach Toe Blake refused to allow Plante to wear it during the game. Three minutes into a game against the New York Rangers, a backhand shot split Plante's lip. He left for a few minutes, and returned wearing a mask.

Goalie Jacques Plante wore the first hockey mask.

● Cristiano Ronaldo of Real Madrid is one of the biggest soccer stars in the world.

What is the world's most popular sport?

You'll get a kick out of this answer! It's soccer—a team sport played in almost every country in the world. More than 3 billion people either play or watch soccer, which is called football everywhere outside the United States. Soccer wasn't very popular in the U.S. until the 1970s. Immigrants to America brought the sport with them and it caught on big time.

Soccer Greats

Voted both Soccer Player of the 20th Century and Athlete of the 20th Century, **Pelé** is the sport's top scorer of all time with more than 1,200 goals. A native of Brazil, Pelé retired from soccer in 1977 after playing in a total of 1,363 games.

Led by **Mia Hamm**, the U.S. women's Olympic soccer team won gold medals in 1996 and 2004. Considered the best female soccer player in the sport's history, Hamm is credited for putting the sport on the map. She scored 158 goals playing against international teams, second-most of all time after fellow U.S. player Abby Wambach. (Pelé scored 77 international goals.)

How are baseball bats made?

When major league baseball players grab a bat in the dugout, more often than not it's a Louisville Slugger. Louisville Sluggers are a big hit with ballplayers—and they have been since the company Hillerich & Bradsby began making wood bats in 1884 in Louisville, Kentucky.

There are dozens of bat companies in the U.S., Canada, and Japan. But Hillerich & Bradsby is the most famous. Over the years, it has sold more than 100,000,000 bats. It sends about 200,000 bats to the pros each year. More than 60 percent of major league players use Louisville Sluggers. To learn how bats are made, you have to head home. Not to home plate, but to the home of the Louisville Slugger.

D YOU KNOW? THE SMALLEST BASEBALL BAT MADE FOR A MAJOR LEAGUER WAS .5 INCHES LONG AND WAS USED BY EARLY PLAYER WEE WILLIE KEELER, WHO WAS 5 FEET, 4.5 INCHES TALL.

1

Every Louisville Slugger starts out as a log cut from trees at one of three mills in the Northeast U.S. One tree can produce 35 to 40 bats. Inside the mill, machines remove bark from the logs, which are cut into 40-inch-long sections.

2

The logs are cut into 18 to 20 smaller tubes, called billets. Billets are damp, so they are dried out in an oven for four to five weeks. The billets are cut down to 37 inches, then shipped to the Louisville Slugger factory in Kentucky.

3

Major league equipment managers send in orders for bats. Players choose specific types of wood (as or maple), shape, length, weight, color, and finish. A machine controlled by a computer shapes the billet into the correct bat model.

4

A player can have his signature stamped on the bat with oil dyes. Or the signature can be burned on with a metal brand heated to 1,400°F. Machines then sand the bat and cut off the knobs, which were used to hold the bat in place.

5

If a bat is colored, it is dipped in paint and hung to dry. Once the bat stops dripping, a special light dries it further for 15 minutes. Now it's ready to be shipped to stadiums around the U.S. and Canada. An average pro player will go through about 100

When was the first Super Bowl?

On January 15, 1967, the champions of the National Football League and the American Football League came together to play the NFL's first championship game. The game, which was played in Los Angeles, California, was called the AFL-NFL World Championship Game. The Green Bay Packers beat the Kansas City Chiefs 35–10.

DID YOU KNOW? THE SUPER BOWL GOT ITS NAME WHEN LAMAR HUNT, THEN THE OWNER OF THE KANSAS CITY CHIEFS, SPIED HIS DAUGHTER PLAYING WITH A SUPER BALL. IT INSPIRED HIM TO CALL THE AFL-NFL WORLD CHAMPIONSHIP GAME THE "SUPER BOWL."

Why are there dimples on golf balls?

Golfers found very early that scuffed-up golf balls flew farther than smooth balls. That's why there are between 300 and 500 dimples on a golf ball. Dimples give a golf ball lift–or height–by creating a layer of fast moving air on the top of the ball and a layer of slower moving air on the bottom of the ball.

Inventions

When was the computer invented?

In 1941, a German engineer named Konrad Zuse built the first working programmable computer. It was called the Z3. Zuse had previously built two other prototypes, the Z1 and Z2. The Z3 did not look anything like modern computers. It was huge—larger than a couple of kitchen tables, and it weighed about a ton. The Z3 operated through a system of mechanical relays and switches. Engineers used this massive computer to help calculate and solve problems related to airplane design.

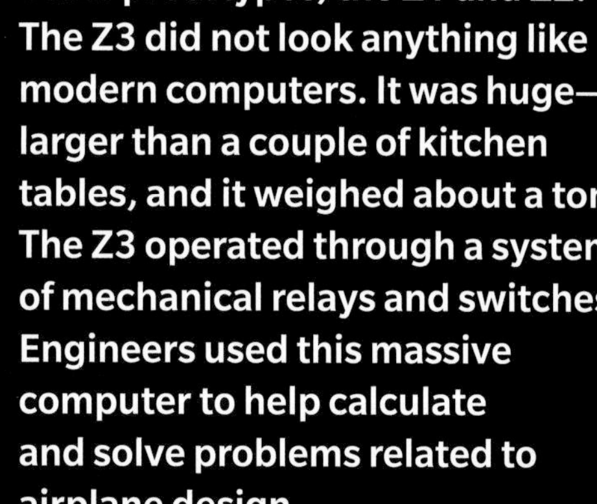

30-Ton Super Brain

In 1943, a company in the United States began building the world's first electronic computer. By November 1945, it unveiled the ENIAC, short for Electronic Numerical Integrator and Computer. Instead of using relays as switches, ENIAC used 18,000 vacuum tubes, similar to the tubes used in the first TV sets. ENIAC weighed 30 tons, but it proved that computers could be indispensable tools.

We've Come a Long Way

Computer technology has changed dramatically over the past decade, and today's tiny processors can be put in anything, anywhere. Futurists predict that with advancing technology, space travel may become commonplace, machines will read our minds, and vehicles will drive themselves.

Where were the transistor and microchip invented?

Before the transistor, vacuum tubes were used in circuits to amplify and control electric signals. But the tubes were large and slow, and quickly burned out. In 1947, at Bell Telephone Laboratories in Murray Hill, New Jersey, scientists Walter Brattain, John Bardeen, and William Shockley figured out how to make crystals perform the same job as vacuum tubes—and transistors were born.

Thanks to that discovery, electrical circuits using transistors could be small, but they still had to be made by hand. In late July 1947, Jack Kilby at Texas Instruments in Dallas had an idea. He thought that it would be easier and cheaper to produce circuits if all the parts were made out of the same material. By September, Kilby had built the first integrated circuit, or microchip. But handwork was still needed to attach the wires that connected the parts.

Just a few months later, Robert Noyce, an engineer at Fairchild Semiconductor in California, found a way to get rid of the wires. Instead, his microchip would use metal lines on top of a protective coating to connect the parts. For the chip, Noyce used silicon, which could handle more power without overheating.

Without these two inventions, there would be no smart phones, digital cameras, MP3 players, or laptop computers. Microchips and their transistors are in almost every electronic device there is, from musical greeting cards to spacecraft.

The first integrated circuit

Robert Noyce with a microchip diagram

What is Djedi?

For hundreds of years, explorers have searched for secret passageways and concealed rooms inside the Great Pyramid of Giza, in Egypt. Now, a robot is finding what no explorer could. The robot, called Djedi, is part of a project led by an international team of researchers.

One of the pyramid's mysteries is what lies in the passageways beyond two eight-inch-square shafts. Because the narrow tunnels climb so high—they are equal to a 13-story building—only a robot can explore the entire length of the tunnel.

In 1993, a different robot reached the end of one of the passageways. But when it drilled through a wall, its camera revealed another wall. Djedi's advanced tools give it greater access, allowing it to explore further.

● The Djedi robot has been exploring the Great Pyramid. The robot found the red markings (below, right). What do they mean?

New Clues to Decode

One of the new robot's features is a snakelike camera, able to fit through small spaces and bend around corners. When Djedi got to the end of a passageway, it pushed its camera through a hole and peeked around the corner. There, it found red hieroglyphs and lines in the stone. The markings were last seen when the pyramid was built, more than 4,500 years ago.

Researchers believe that if the hieroglyphs can be deciphered, they may explain why the tunnels were built. What other secrets are hiding beyond a long shaft or behind a stone door? Perhaps a small robot will reveal the answers.

● The Great Pyramid at Giza is the largest of Egypt's 70 pyramids. When it was built around 2550 B.C., it was about 480 feet high.

Why did scientists create a robot that can play soccer?

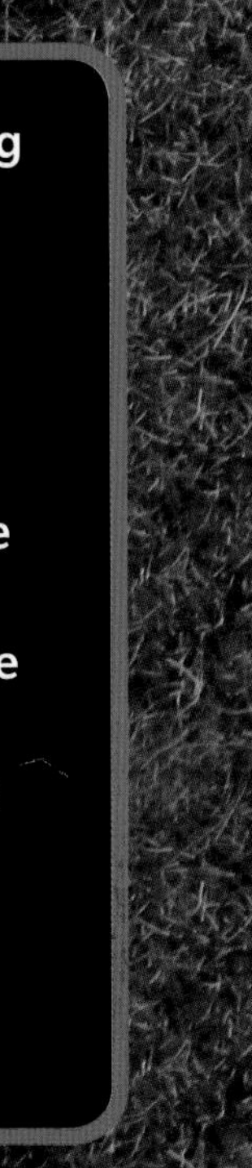

Scientists are designing a robot that can copy human movements. They chose soccer because the moves are complex and it's so popular around the world. CHARLI-2 is a full-size humanoid designed to run, kick, and balance, seeing the soccer field and opponents around it. Though CHARLI-2 is made of lightweight materials, it is still stiff and slow compared to human soccer stars.

Why is the printing press one of the most important inventions of all time?

You probably think your iPod, iPhone, or your laptop are the most important inventions in the history of the world. Think again! Most people say the invention of the printing press was way more important. Prior to the mid-1400s, there was only one way to print a book—by hand. It was a long, hard, and expensive process. Only a few books existed, and only rich people could afford them. That all changed when Johannes Gutenberg, a German inventor, invented the printing press in 1440. The press made it easier to print books, and more people learned to read.

DID YOU KNOW? THE FIRST BOOK TO ROLL OFF THE GUTENBERG PRINTING PRESS WAS THE BIBLE. NO ONE KNOWS HOW MANY GUTENBERG PRINTED, BUT SOME GUESS HE PRODUCED AT LEAST 180 VOLUMES. SOME OF GUTENBERG'S BIBLES STILL EXIST TODAY.

What are some foods invented by accident?

Many discoveries come about by accident or by an out-and-out mistake. When that happens with food inventions, the results are often lip-smacking good.

What: Corn Flakes
Who: John Harvey Kellogg and Will Keith Kellogg
When: 1894
Where: Battle Creek, Michigan

Waste not; want not. That's what the Kellogg brothers, who ran a home for people in poor health, believed. So when Will left some boiled wheat sitting out and it went stale, the two men attempted to turn it into long sheets of dough. Instead, the wheat came out of the rollers in flakes, which the brothers toasted and served to their patients. The cereal was a hit. Later, the brothers tried their new technique on other grains, including corn.

What: Chocolate Chip Cookies
Who: Ruth Wakefield, innkeeper | When: 1930
Where: Toll House Inn, Whitman, Massachusetts

One day, Ruth Wakefield ran out of baking chocolate while preparing a batch of cookies for her guests. All she had on hand was a chocolate candy bar, so she broke it up and added the pieces to her batter. She expected the chocolate to melt evenly. Instead, the cookies were studded with gooey bits of chocolate, and a new treat was born.

What: Potato Chips
Who: George Crum
When: 1853
Where: Moon Lake House, Saratoga Springs, New York

Customers can be tough to please. Chef George Crum knew that all too well. A guest at his inn kept returning his fried potatoes, claiming they weren't crisp enough, so the chef sliced a new batch of potatoes as thin as he could, fried them in oil, and sprinkled salt on them. The dish wasn't returned and soon others wanted their potatoes made the same way.

What: Ice-Cream Cones
Who: Ernest Hamwi
When: 1904
Where: World's Fair, St. Louis, Missouri

Arnold Fornachou, a vendor at the fair, had just run out of paper dishes to serve his ice cream, and customers were lining up. He turned to his fellow vendors for help. Ernest Hamwi came to the rescue. He rolled up his waffle-like pastries and gave them to Fornachou to fill with ice cream. Later, Hamwi received a patent for a pastry cone-making machine and started his own company.

Workers show off some of the toys and other wood products produced by LEGO in 1932.

Where were LEGO bricks invented?

In 1932, a carpenter named Ole Kirk Kristiansen started a company in Billund, Denmark, that made wood stepladders, ironing boards, and toys. He named the company LEGO, a word formed by combining the first two letters of leg and godt, the Danish words for "play well." Soon, Kristiansen was making only high-quality toys out of wood. After World War II, LEGO started producing plastic toys. In 1949, the company launched Automatic Binding Bricks, its first interlocking construction blocks.

In the 1950s, the name was changed to LEGO bricks, and the company came out with the LEGO System of Play, which included 28 sets and 8 vehicles. It also began selling the toys outside of Denmark for the first time. In 1958, LEGO received a patent for the modern bricks so famous today. The new bricks not only had studs on top, but tubes inside that lock onto the studs of other bricks and hold them securely together.

Today, the company produces billions of LEGO parts a year. They are sold all over the world. In fact, enough LEGO Bricks are sold every year to circle the world five times if laid end to end!

Play Value

New York City's Nathan Sawaya is proof that you can have fun and make a living at the same time. In 2004, he gave up his job as a lawyer to become a full-time artist—making sculptures out of regular LEGO bricks you can buy in any toy store. But Sawaya buys them by the thousands. In fact, he has about 1.5 million in his studio! Among his creations is a 20-foot-long Tyrannosaurus rex (right).

When was the first successful telephone call?

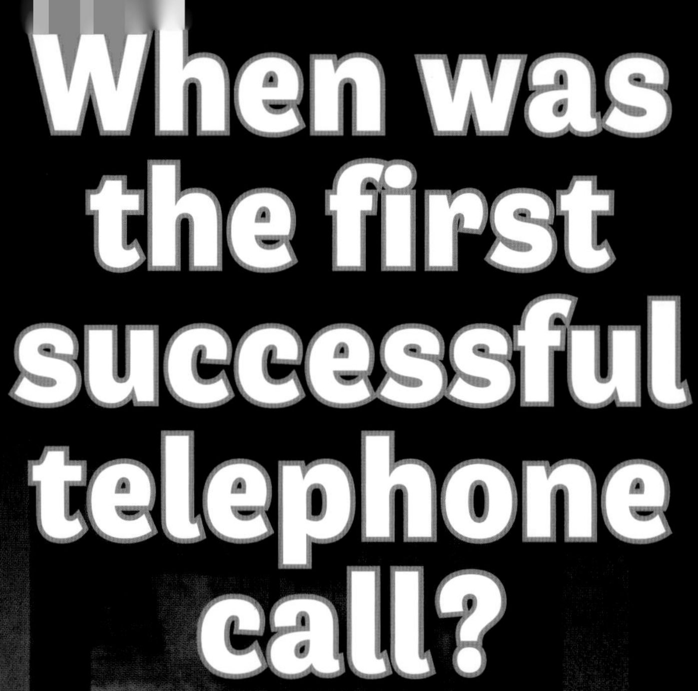

Alexander Graham Bell believed there had to be a different, better way to communicate across distances. He invented a machine that used electricity to transmit human voices over a wire. He called it the "electrical speech machine." We call it the telephone.

"Mr. Watson, come here!"

On March 10, 1876, Bell sat in his workshop and fiddled with his invention. When he was ready, he told his assistant, Thomas Watson, to go into another room. Bell spoke into the mouthpiece, "Mr. Watson, come here! I want to see you." When Watson heard Bell, he came running, excited that Bell's "electrical speech machine" actually worked.

A Toy?

Most people thought Bell's telephone was interesting, but nothing more than a toy. Bell knew better. He told his father that he could foresee the day when "friends converse with each other without leaving home." By 1905, there were more than 2 million phones in the United States. While the design and technology have changed, the purpose remains basically the same.

Phone Evolution

A Look At How Phones Have Changed Over the Years

How does a microwave oven cook food?

There's fast food. And then there's faster food. A microwave oven can heat up some foods in a minute or less. A microwave oven cooks with a type of radiation called microwaves, which are similar to the waves that transmit TV. Microwaves don't heat air. Instead, they penetrate food, making the food's water and fat molecules vibrate. The vibrations produce heat in a jiffy. Microwaves don't heat up plastic, ceramics, paper, or glass. So, food in a microwave often sits on plates made of these materials. When you pull out a cool plate from a microwave, it can fool you into thinking the food isn't hot. But it is—so be careful before you take a bite!

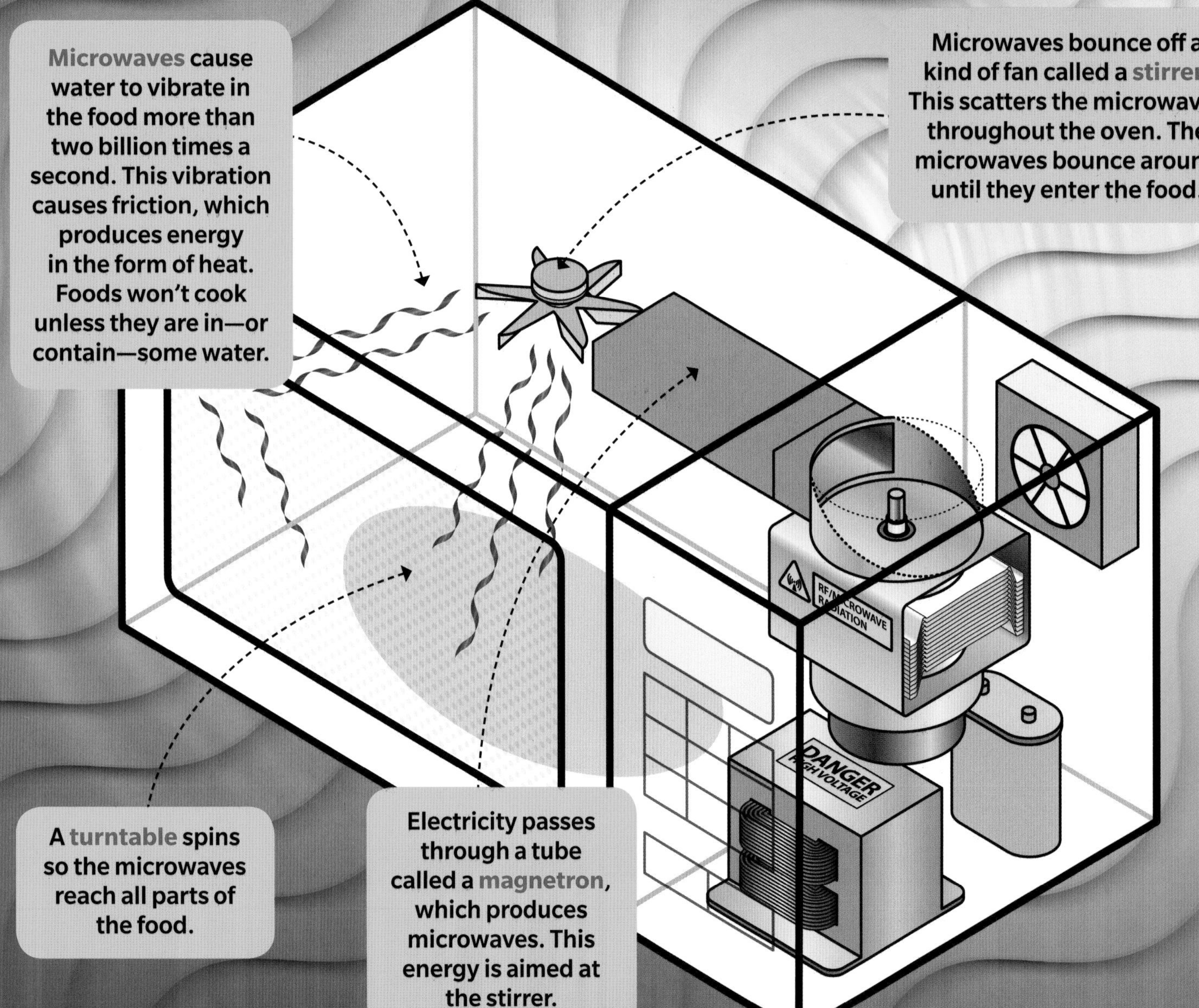

Microwaves cause water to vibrate in the food more than two billion times a second. This vibration causes friction, which produces energy in the form of heat. Foods won't cook unless they are in—or contain—some water.

Microwaves bounce off a kind of fan called a **stirrer**. This scatters the microwaves throughout the oven. The microwaves bounce around until they enter the food.

A **turntable** spins so the microwaves reach all parts of the food.

Electricity passes through a tube called a **magnetron**, which produces microwaves. This energy is aimed at the stirrer.

When was the first e-mail sent?

An Electronic Revolution

It takes time to write a letter, mail it, and wait for a reply. E-mail allows people to communicate instantly. More than 1 billion people send e-mails every day. Today's e-mails include different kinds of attachments, including documents, videos, and pictures.

In 1971, Ray Tomlinson, a computer engineer working on what would become the Internet, sent the first e-mail—short for "electronic mail." While working on the Internet project, Tomlinson realized that there had to be a better way to leave messages on the computers of other scientists.

Tomlinson solved the problem by using the @ sign to target other computers on the system. The @ sign allowed Tomlinson to separate a computer user's address from the name of the network they were on. He began by sending messages between two computers that weren't that far apart. No one—not even Tomlinson—remembers what that historic message said.

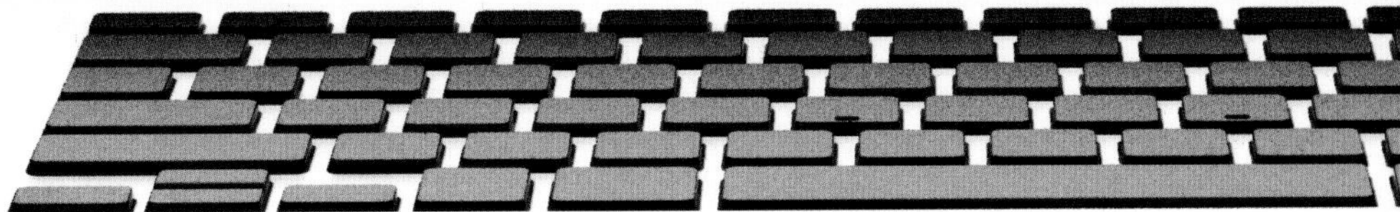

Geography

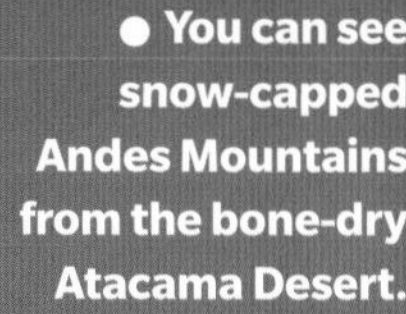

● You can see snow-capped Andes Mountains from the bone-dry Atacama Desert.

Where is the driest place on Earth?

The driest place on Earth is a city in Chile, South America, called Arica, which once went 14 years without a single drop of rain. The average amount of precipitation that falls is a measly 0.03 inches. Arica is located in the world's driest desert—the Atacama.

The desert covers more than 600 miles. In this desolate area, you won't see plants or animals, just vast stretches of empty land. One region has soil that is similar to the kind found on Mars. In fact, sci-fi directors sometimes film in the Atacama.

● Nets like these help collect water droplets in the fog.

● Plants in the Atacama Desert get the water they need by taking in moisture from fog.

Even though the Atacama Desert is such a harsh environment, there are towns and farms. How do people survive? Some communities transported water by truck, but that was very expensive. Today, they make use of a marine fog called *camanchaca* (ka-men-*chak*-a). Scientists found a way to collect the dense fog that forms on Chile's Pacific coast and drifts inland over the desert. People hang netting, which captures the water droplets in the fog. The droplets condense and drip into basins. The water is then piped to villages in the area. In the village of Chungungo, this system supplies the residents with more than 2,500 gallons of water each day.

Why don't penguins live at the North Pole?

Penguins can live at the South Pole because way down under the thick ice, there's land. The land means the ice is stable, so penguins can tend their nests, make shelter, and otherwise survive when they're not in the ocean. Since the North Pole is made of floating ice that is always moving and shifting, it's not the best place to call home.

Why is Easter Island called Easter Island?

● Natives of Easter Island carved these human figures out of stone hundreds of years ago.

The island, located in the Pacific Ocean about 2,300 miles (3,701 km) off the coast of Chile, got its name because a Dutch admiral landed there on Easter day in 1722. Can you guess why Christmas Island in Australia is called Christmas Island?

When was the Great Wall of China built?

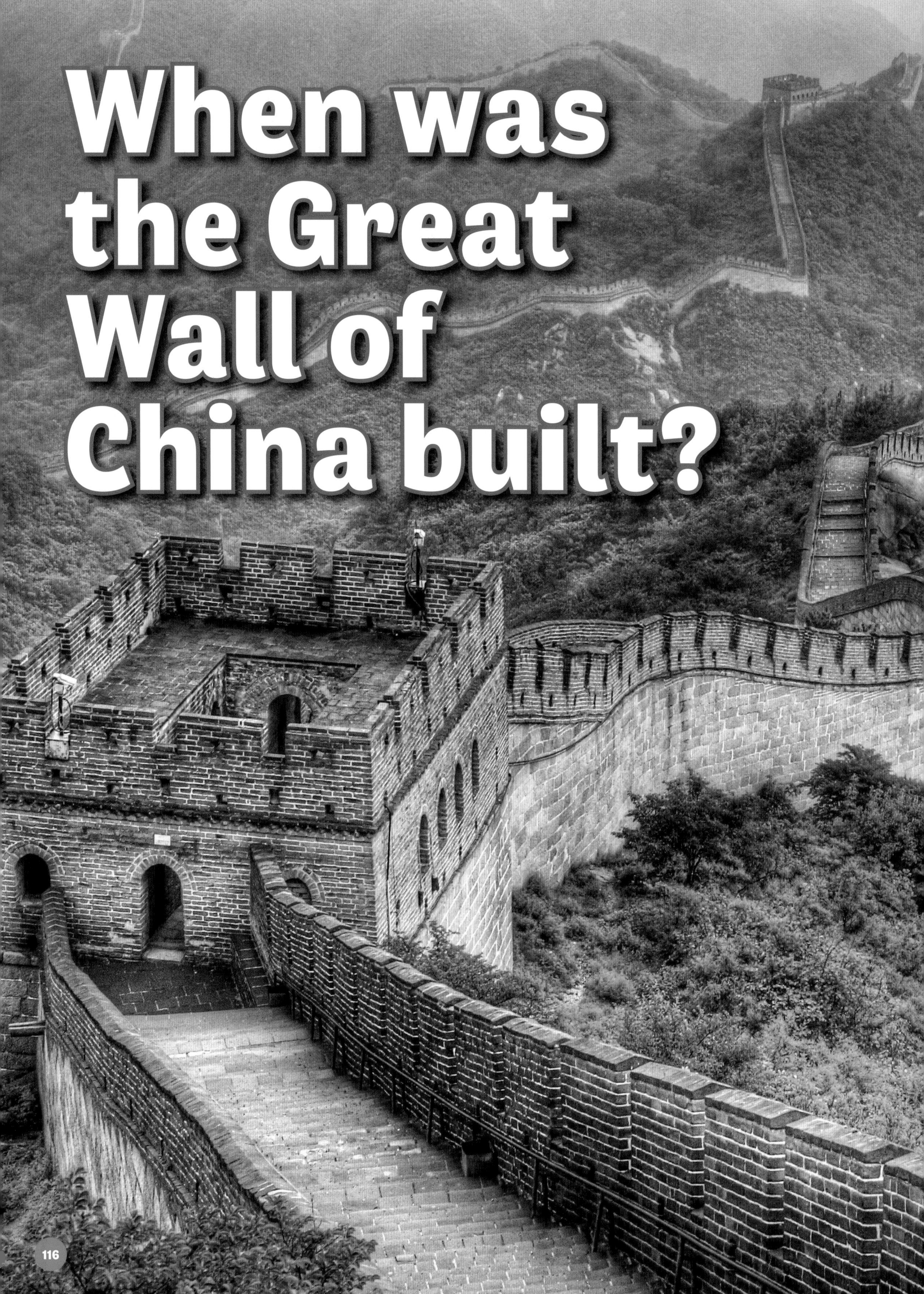

DID YOU KNOW? THE CHINESE BUILT MUCH OF THE WALL BY POUNDING DIRT BETWEEN BOARD FRAMES. EXPERTS ESTIMATE THAT WORKERS USED ROUGHLY 393 MILLION CUBIC YARDS OF DIRT DURING CONSTRUCTION. THEY ALSO BUILT PARTS OF THE WALL FROM BRICK AND STONE.

The Great Wall of China was built about 2,500 years ago. It is actually a series of walls that stretch for about 5,000 miles (8,047 km). China's first emperor connected several walls in the northern part of the country to defend against outside attacks. The Great Wall of China has been called the "longest cemetery on Earth" due to the number of people who died during its construction—possibly over 1 million. To save funeral and burial expenses, the bodies were buried in the wall.

Where can you find fairy chimneys and underground cities?

Cappadocia in central Turkey is a magical landscape of fairy chimneys, cones, and rippled valleys as well as rock houses and ancient underground settlements. They are all carved out of tuff. This soft rock was formed from thick layers of ash left behind by volcanoes millions of years ago. Over a long time, rains and melting snow eroded the tuff, sculpting it into the shapes that attract tourists from all over the world.

About 3,500 years ago, people began making their homes out of the rock. Over the centuries, they built more than 35 underground cities. The cities provided shelter as well as a place for people to hide from enemies. One of the largest cities is Kaymakli, which has eight floors, staircases, ventilation shafts, and almost 100 tunnels.

● Rooms and tunnels in the underground city of Kaymakli in Cappadocia

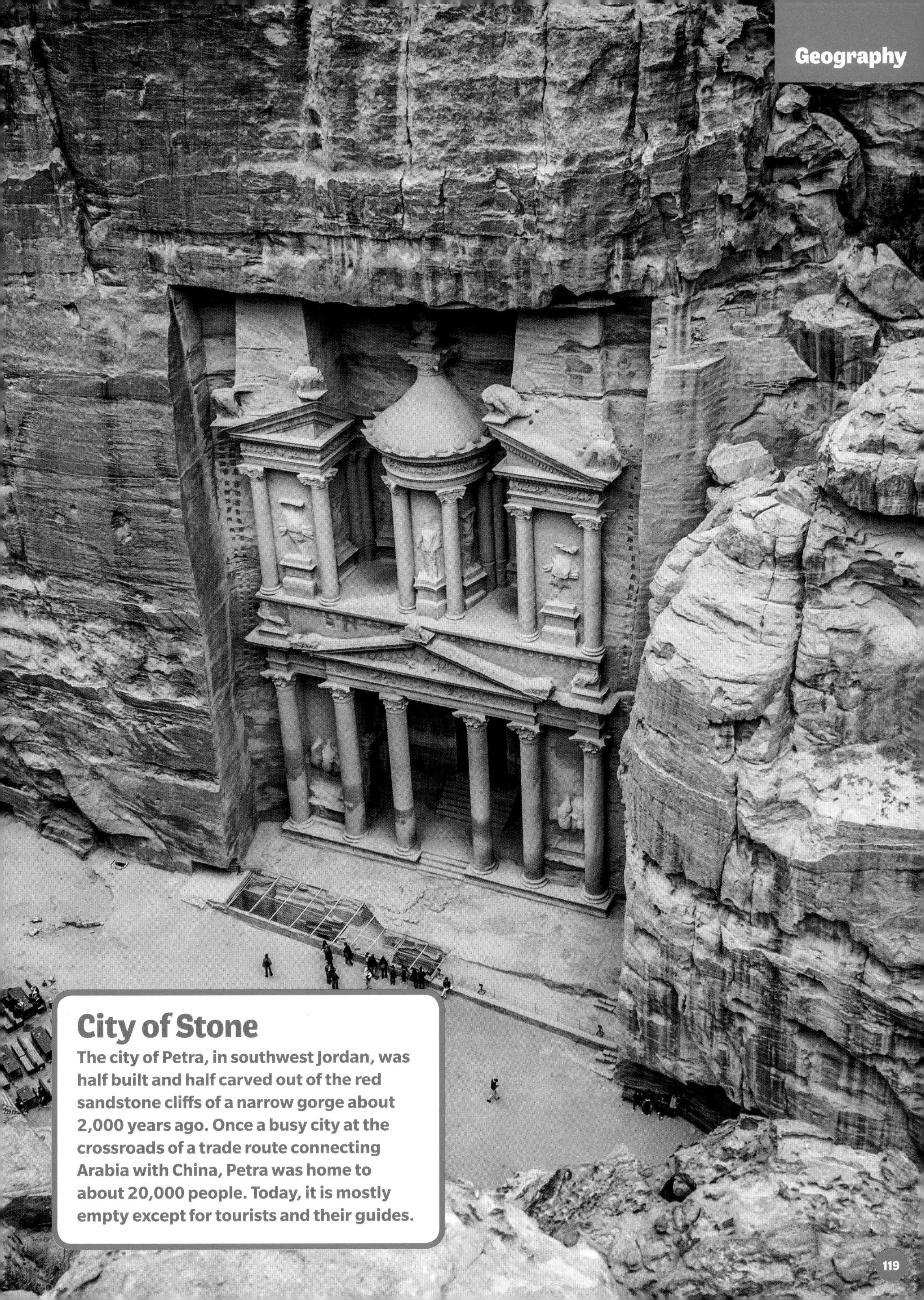

City of Stone

The city of Petra, in southwest Jordan, was half built and half carved out of the red sandstone cliffs of a narrow gorge about 2,000 years ago. Once a busy city at the crossroads of a trade route connecting Arabia with China, Petra was home to about 20,000 people. Today, it is mostly empty except for tourists and their guides.

Where are the highest tides in the world?

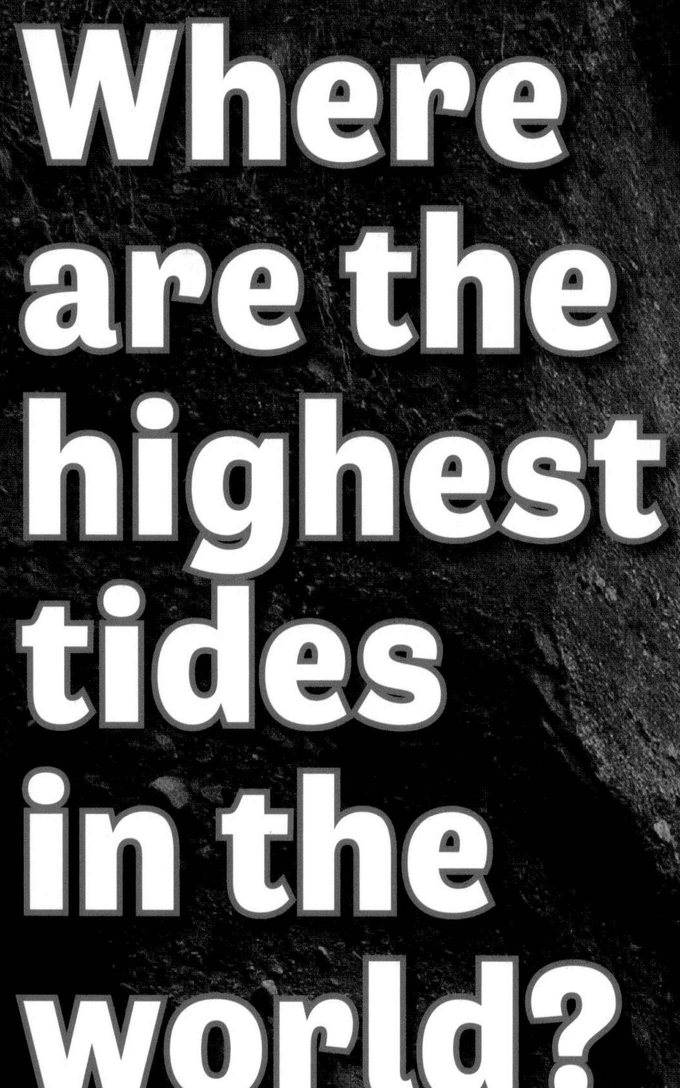

● At low tide, people can walk around sea stacks carved by the ocean. But they have to be careful not to get caught there when the tide comes in (above).

High tides in Canada's Bay of Fundy can reach about 56 feet—higher than a five-story building. The funnel-shaped bay becomes narrower and shallower along its length, forcing the water higher and higher up the shore. At the head of the bay, Minas Basin has the highest tides.

The length of the tidal cycle—one high tide and one low tide—is 12 hours and 26 minutes. So twice a day, more than 120 billion tons of water flow in and out of the 174-mile-long bay. That's equal to the daily flow of water in all the rivers of the world combined!

Surging tides stir up nutrients from the seafloor and marshes, providing food for an incredible number of animals, from sea slugs to fish, seals, whales, and more than 300 species of birds. Among these are millions of migrating seabirds that flock to the bay's mudflats to dine on tiny animals called mud shrimp.

Tourists also flock to the Bay of Fundy. They go to see the changing tides and whirlpools, to explore the mudflats and look at the sea stacks shaped by the tides, to hunt fossils, and to enjoy bird- and whale-watching.

● Global warming affects the homes of many animals, including polar bears.

What is global warming?

The Earth's average temperature is gradually rising. Year by year it is heating up. By 2100, many scientists predict that our planet's overall temperature will be from 2°F to 11.5°F higher than it is today. That might not sound like much, but only a difference of 9°F separates our time from the Ice Age.

Why is Earth getting hotter? Many scientists think burning fossil fuels, such as gasoline and coal, are to blame. The fuels give off carbon dioxide which rises into the atmosphere. This traps the sun's heat so it can't escape back into space. Global warming disrupts the climate and its weather patterns.

Why doesn't Niagara Falls freeze in winter?

With 150,000 gallons of water going over the falls every second, it's nearly impossible for Niagara Falls or the Niagara River to freeze over. However, an ice bridge often forms at the base of the falls and over a part of the Niagara River below the falls.

Which country is made up of more than 17,500 islands?

Sumatra

The Republic of Indonesia is the world's largest group of islands. The bigger islands include Sumatra, Java, Sulawesi, about three-quarters of Borneo (also called Kalimantan), and half of New Guinea. Among the smaller islands are Bali, which is famous for its beautiful white-sand beaches, and the Moluccas, which were once called the Spice Islands.

Indonesia has about 76 active volcanoes, more than anywhere else on Earth. It is home to the Komodo dragon, the largest lizard, as well as the world's largest flower. The Rafflesia arnoldii flower can be up to three feet across and weigh as much as 15 pounds. The Titan arum is even bigger—up to 12 feet high and 170 pounds—but its blossom is not one but thousands of tiny flowers.

The Komodo dragon can grow up to 10 feet long and weigh more than 300 pounds.

The Titan arum is also called the corpse flower because it smells so bad.

Volcanoes can be found in Bromo Tengger Semeru National Park on the island of Java.

The Rafflesia arnoldii plant is a parasite: it attaches itself to another plant and steals its water and nutrients.

Why is Mount Everest so tall?

Some 250 million years ago, India, Africa, Australia, and South America were all one continent that scientists call Pangea. About 60 million years ago, the tectonic plate that India sits on moved northward, charging across the equator at roughly 5.91 inches (15 cm) a year. Eventually, India slammed into Asia. The collision erased an ocean named the Tethys Sea. The colliding plates and the sinking ocean floor pushed up the Himalaya Mountains, including what became Mount Everest, the tallest mountain in the world.

Why is the Grand Canyon so huge?

A canyon is a deep, narrow valley with steep sides. The Grand Canyon, in Arizona, is more than one mile (1.6 km) deep in places. Its upper rim measures an average of 10 miles (16 km) from edge to edge. The rushing Colorado River carved out this amazing spectacle over millions of years. During that time, the river washed away tremendous amounts of rocks and dirt, leaving behind this cavernous canyon.

Human Body

What is the strongest muscle in your body?

Of the more than 600 muscles in the human body, which one deserves the title of strongest? The answer isn't simple. It all depends on how you define strength. Some muscles have greater endurance or work harder, but when it comes to pure brute force, one muscle rules. Chew on this—it's the jaw muscle. The human jaw can chomp down with a force of up to 200 pounds. It would be the same as having a 200-pound weight coming down on an object. In theory, the jaw is capable of crushing its own teeth.

Other Strong Muscles

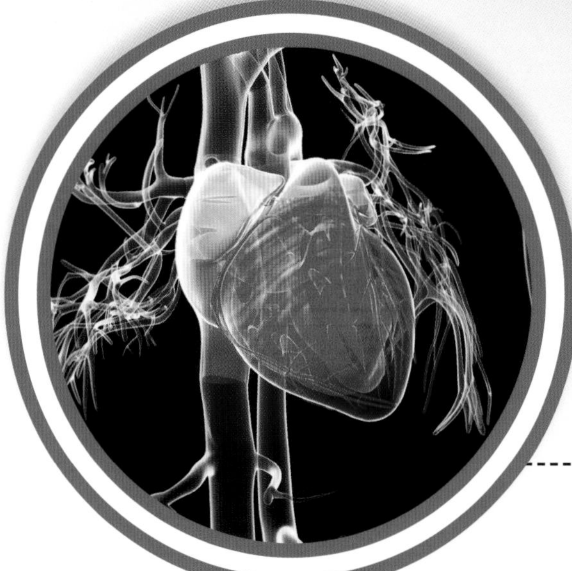

◂ Pump It Up

The heart, which works 24/7, is the body's hardest-working muscle. With each heartbeat, it pumps 2 ounces of blood and at least 2,500 gallons of blood daily.

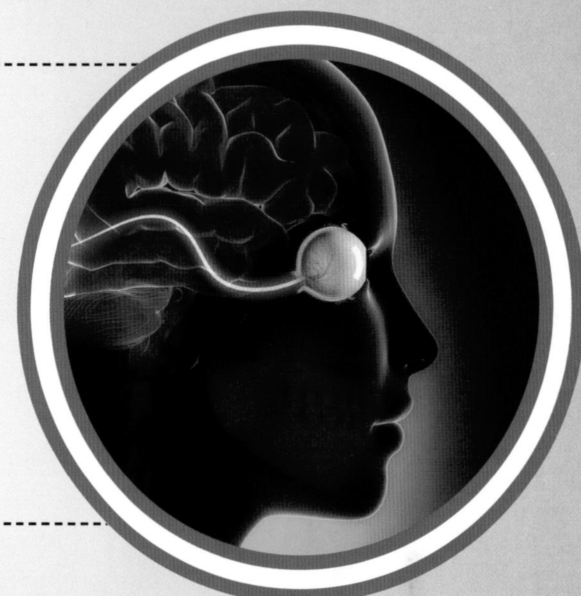

Always Moving ▸

Among the smallest muscles in the body, the eye muscles are also some of the strongest. They have great elastic strength and can exert force quickly. When reading, your eyes make more than 10,000 tiny movements per hour.

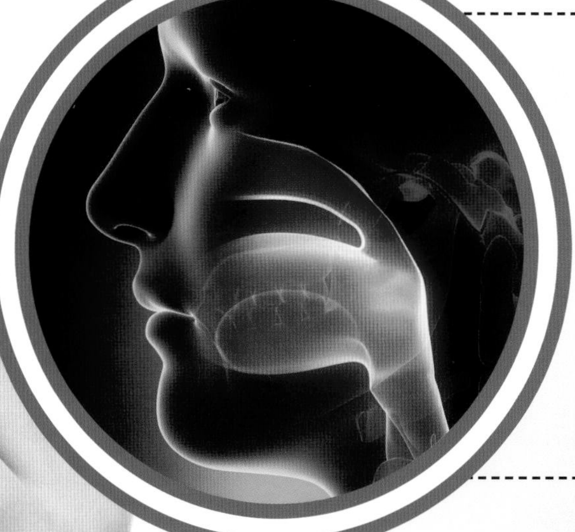

◂ Tongue Twister

Another tough worker is the tongue. Actually a group of muscles, the tongue never quits. It's at work when we eat, speak, and sleep. That's right. At night while we snooze, the tongue pushes saliva into the throat. If you want to see how strong it is, try forcing your tongue down with your finger.

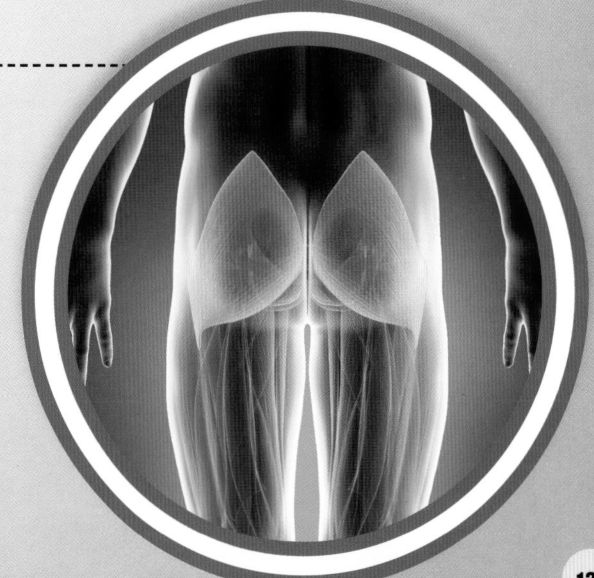

Be Seated ▸

The gluteus maximus—the muscles in the butt—is the body's largest muscle and one of its strongest. It keeps your trunk (the main part of the body from the stomach up to the head) erect.

What is the brain made of?

Your brain is the commander-in-chief of your body. It tells your heart to beat, your lungs to breathe, and your eyes to blink. The human brain is the most complex human organ. Billions of nerve cells, called neurons, make up the brain. These neurons are connected, constantly interacting with each other as they send messages to all the cells in the body.

If you look at a neuron up close, you can see that it branches off into lots of long spindly ends. One extra-long branch is called the axon. The shorter ones are dendrites. These nerve endings connect to other neurons, passing on and receiving information in the form of electrical signals. The axon sends out signals, while the dendrites receive signals from other neurons.

DID YOU KNOW? OUR BRAINS ARE FOLDED IN ORDER TO SAVE SPACE AND SQUEEZE IN AS MUCH CORTEX AREA AS POSSIBLE. IF OUR BRAINS WERE SMOOTH, OUR HEADS WOULD HAVE TO BE THE SIZE OF BEACH BALLS!

Neurons don't touch one another. Instead they connect by jumping across synapses, tiny gaps between the cells. A synapse releases chemicals that travel across a gap and trigger an electrical impulse in the next neuron.

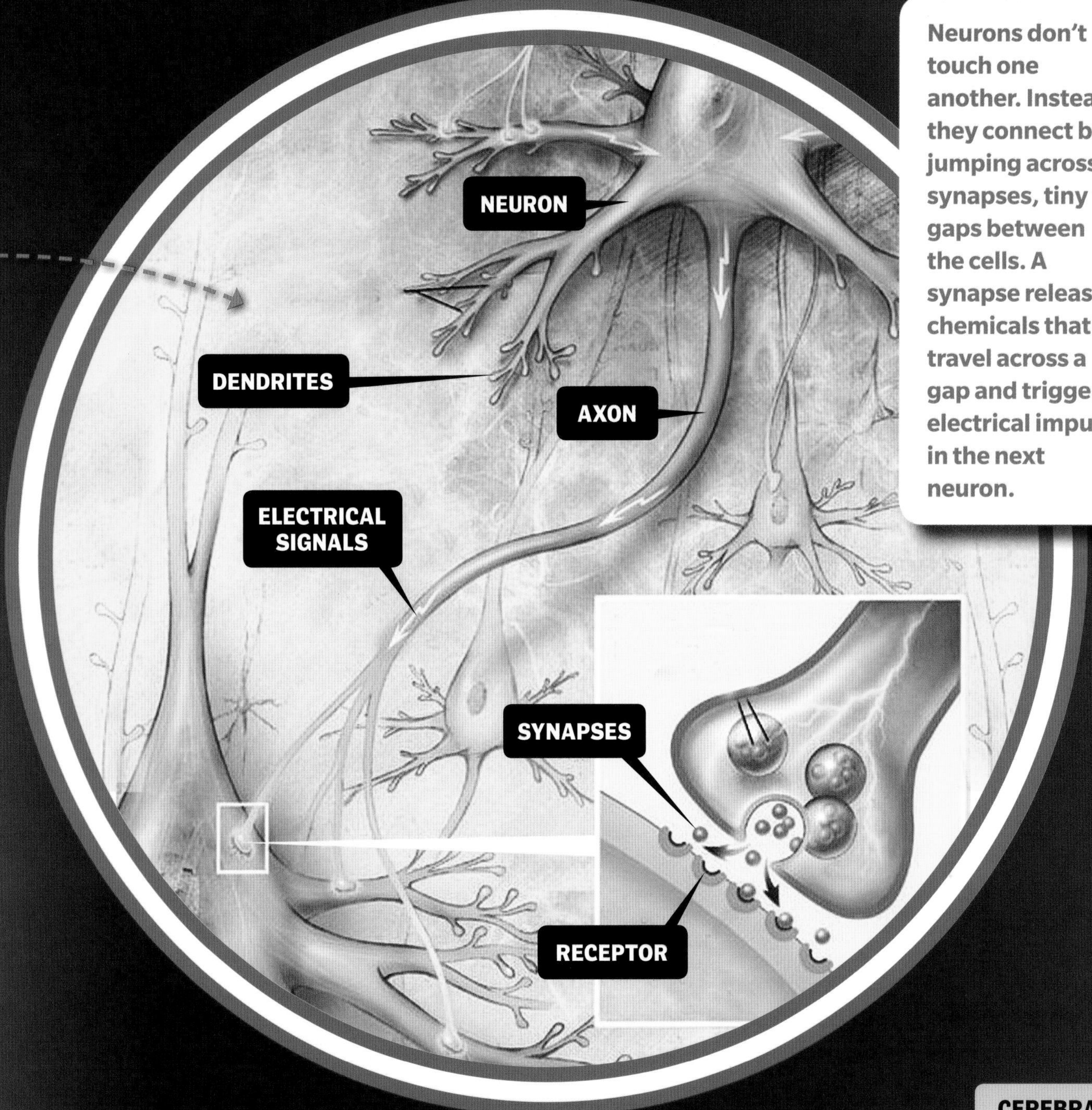

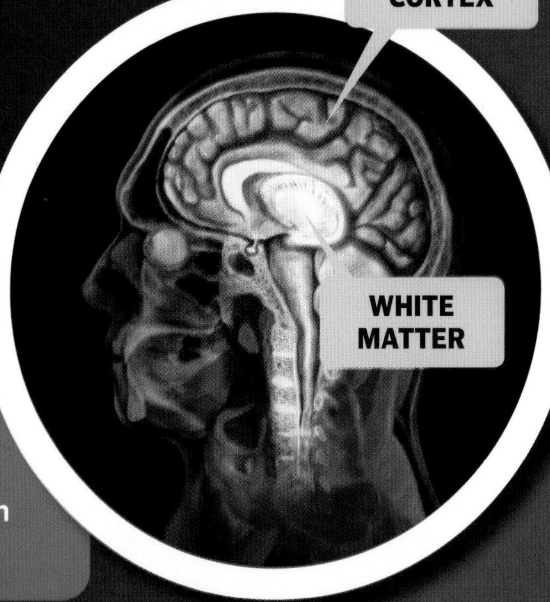

A Look Inside

The outer part of the brain, called the **cerebral cortex**, is grayish in color and has deep folds. This area, where most of our thinking takes place, is extremely dense with dendrites. The inner area of the brain is paler in color and known as **white matter**. It's mostly made up of axons. Axons are covered with a fatty substance called myelin sheath, which gives the inner brain its whitish color.

Why do some people go bald?

Homer Simpson used to have a full head of hair. But every time Marge told her husband that she was going to have a baby, TV's favorite cartoon dad yanked out whatever curls he had. Luckily, most people don't go bald this way. Baldness is caused by a person's genes and hormones. Genes are inherited characteristics such as eye and hair color. Hormones control how the body functions. The actual process of going bald, however, remains a mystery—except if you're Homer Simpson. Chances are if you are a guy and your dad has gone bald, you probably will too at his age!

Why do teeth get cavities?

When you eat sugar, it stays on your teeth even after you finish the food. But the eating isn't done: bacteria in your mouth eats away at the sugar. As bacteria eat, they change the sugar to plaque, which in turn eats into your teeth. The places where plaque stays too long become the holes we call cavities.

How do we cry?

When you see a sad movie, you cry. When a piece of dust gets in your eye, you shed tears. Our eyes can turn into a water fountain pretty easily. Even when we're not crying, tears are constantly being produced. Every time we blink, we spread tears over our eyes. This type of tears is produced slowly and steadily. They keep our eyes smooth, clear, and free of bits of dust and pollen. Tears also keep our eyes healthy. They contain salt and proteins that nourish the eye, and a chemical called lysozyme (*lie*-suh-zyme) that fights germs.

If an eye gets irritated, the tear glands produce a flood of tears. This can happen when wind, smoke, or fumes strike our eyeballs. People also cry when they are sad, happy, or in pain. Tears produced by strong emotions contain hormones produced in the body. Crying washes away these hormones—and sometimes makes you feel better.

DID YOU KNOW? HUMANS AREN'T THE ONLY ANIMALS TO SHED TEARS. MOST MAMMALS HAVE TEAR GLANDS THAT WORK LIKE OURS TO CLEAN AND KEEP EYES MOIST.

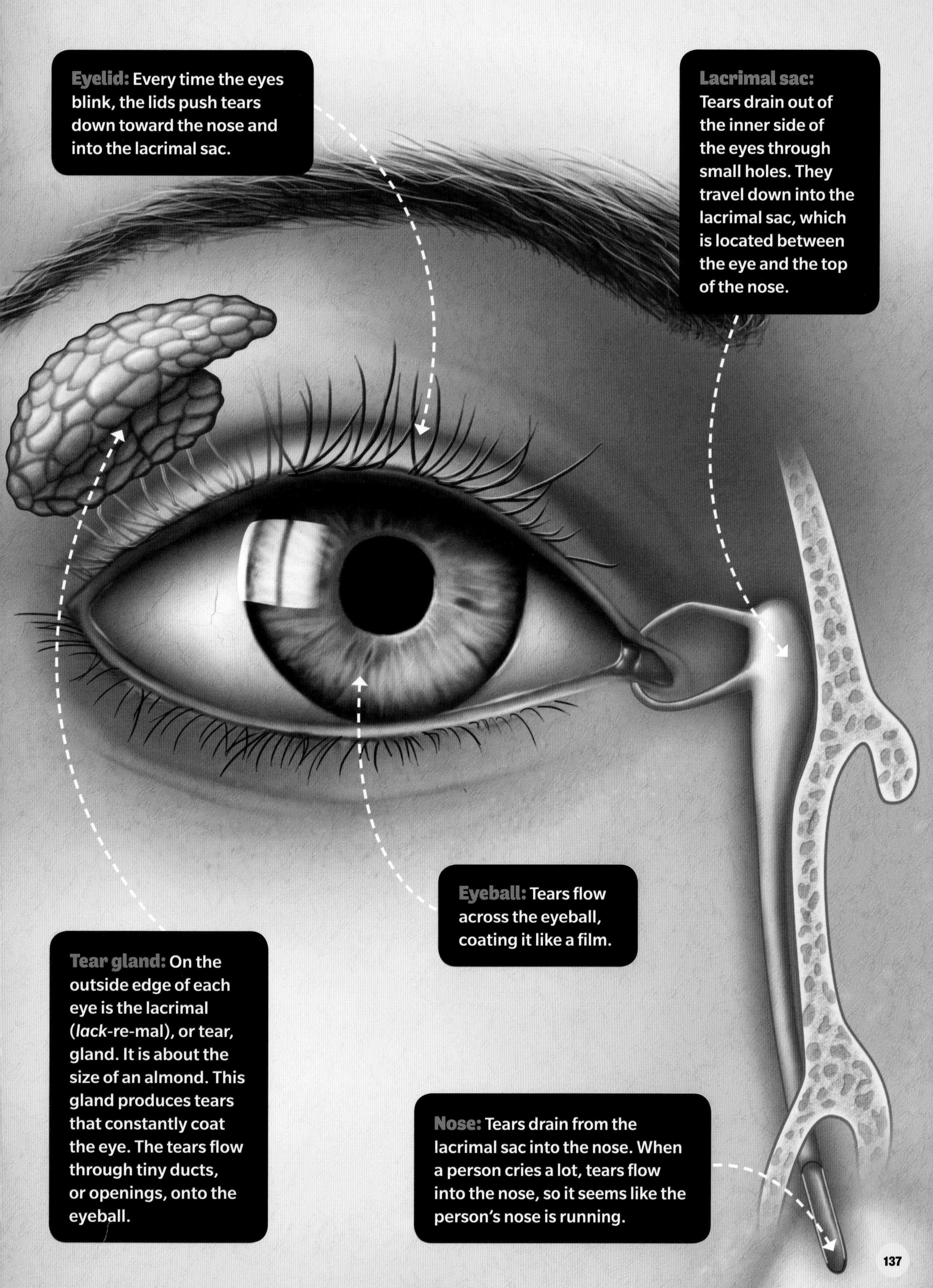
Eyelid: Every time the eyes blink, the lids push tears down toward the nose and into the lacrimal sac.
Lacrimal sac: Tears drain out of the inner side of the eyes through small holes. They travel down into the lacrimal sac, which is located between the eye and the top of the nose.
Eyeball: Tears flow across the eyeball, coating it like a film.
Tear gland: On the outside edge of each eye is the lacrimal (*lack*-re-mal), or tear, gland. It is about the size of an almond. This gland produces tears that constantly coat the eye. The tears flow through tiny ducts, or openings, onto the eyeball.
Nose: Tears drain from the lacrimal sac into the nose. When a person cries a lot, tears flow into the nose, so it seems like the person's nose is running.

When did people first talk?

It's hard to say when humans first developed a spoken language, but most scholars agree it was about 150,000 years ago. Some historians suspect humans began talking nonstop some 40,000 years ago, when the first artistic cave paintings and musical instruments came on the scene.

● This cave painting was created about 15,000 years ago.

What Is Language?

Dolphins squeak, click, whistle, and squawk. Honeybees dance to let other bees know where to find pollen. Birds sing. Dogs bark. These animals can communicate. But humans are the only social animals that have developed a complex spoken language. Language is a shared, organized system of sounds, words, and sentences. People use language to communicate what they are thinking. Language also allows people to pass down their history and culture to the next generation.

Say Again?

¿Habla usted español? Parlez-vous français? Sprechen Sie Deutsch? Do you recognize these phrases in Spanish, French, and German? There are about 6,900 languages in the world. Languages spread when people move from place to place. As people settle in their new homes, they take their language with them.

DID YOU KNOW? HALF OF THE WORLD'S LANGUAGES WILL BE EXTINCT BY 2115. ONE REASON FOR THIS IS THAT FEWER YOUNG PEOPLE ARE LEARNING NATIVE LANGUAGES FROM THEIR PARENTS.

Why do I have two lungs?

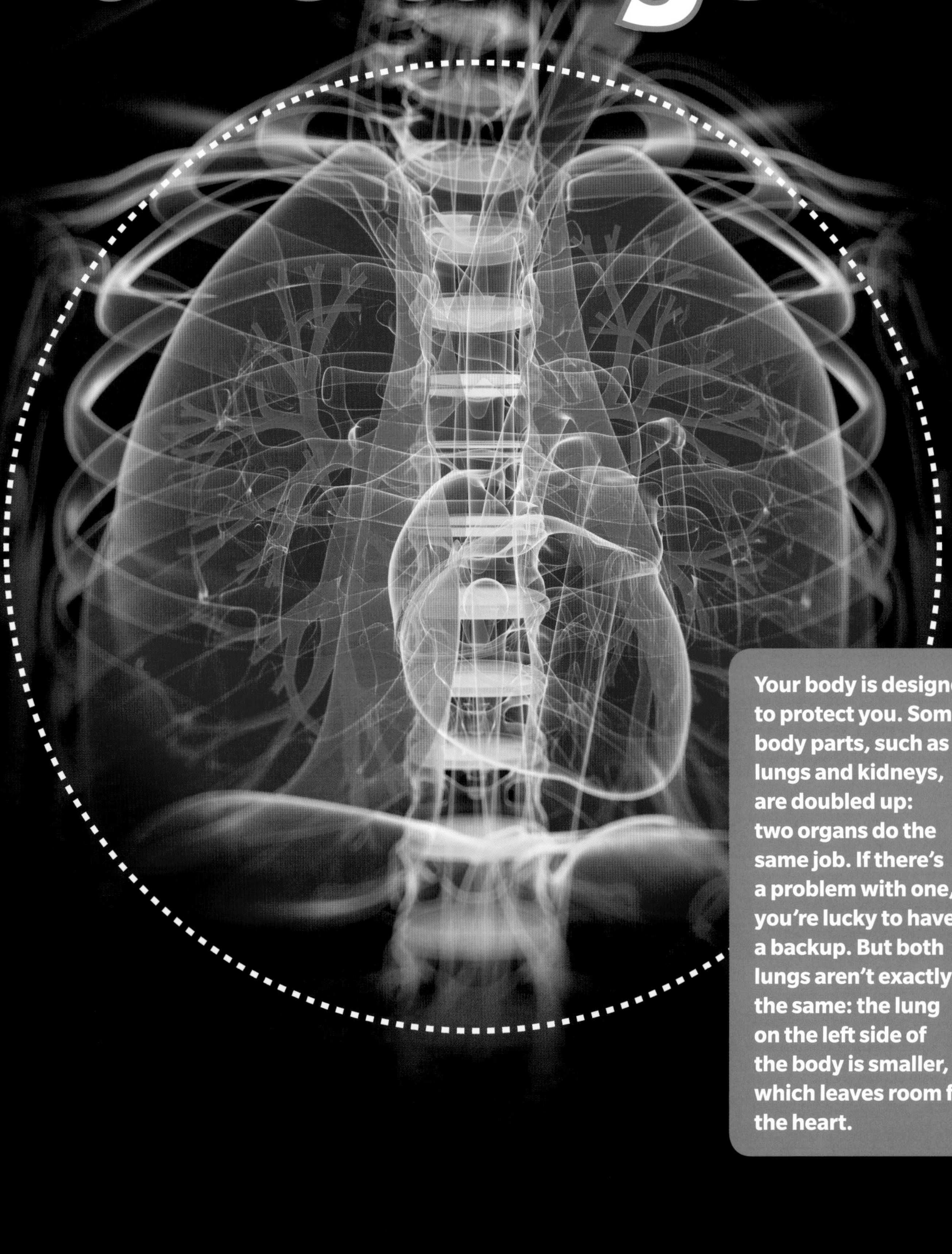

Your body is designed to protect you. Some body parts, such as lungs and kidneys, are doubled up: two organs do the same job. If there's a problem with one, you're lucky to have a backup. But both lungs aren't exactly the same: the lung on the left side of the body is smaller, which leaves room for the heart.

How does loud music hurt your hearing?

You've probably heard that listening to iPods and MP3 players through earbuds at high volume can hurt your hearing. Unfortunately, people who hear the warnings don't always turn down the volume. Some people think the maximum setting on an iPod is safe. But at the highest volume, some music players are as loud as a chainsaw or rock concert.

Researchers have found that listening with earbuds or in-ear headphones to music at full blast for just five minutes a day can, over time, cause permanent hearing loss. Listening at a high volume an hour a day can damage your hearing after five years. So when you're listening to music, turn down the volume.

How We Hear:

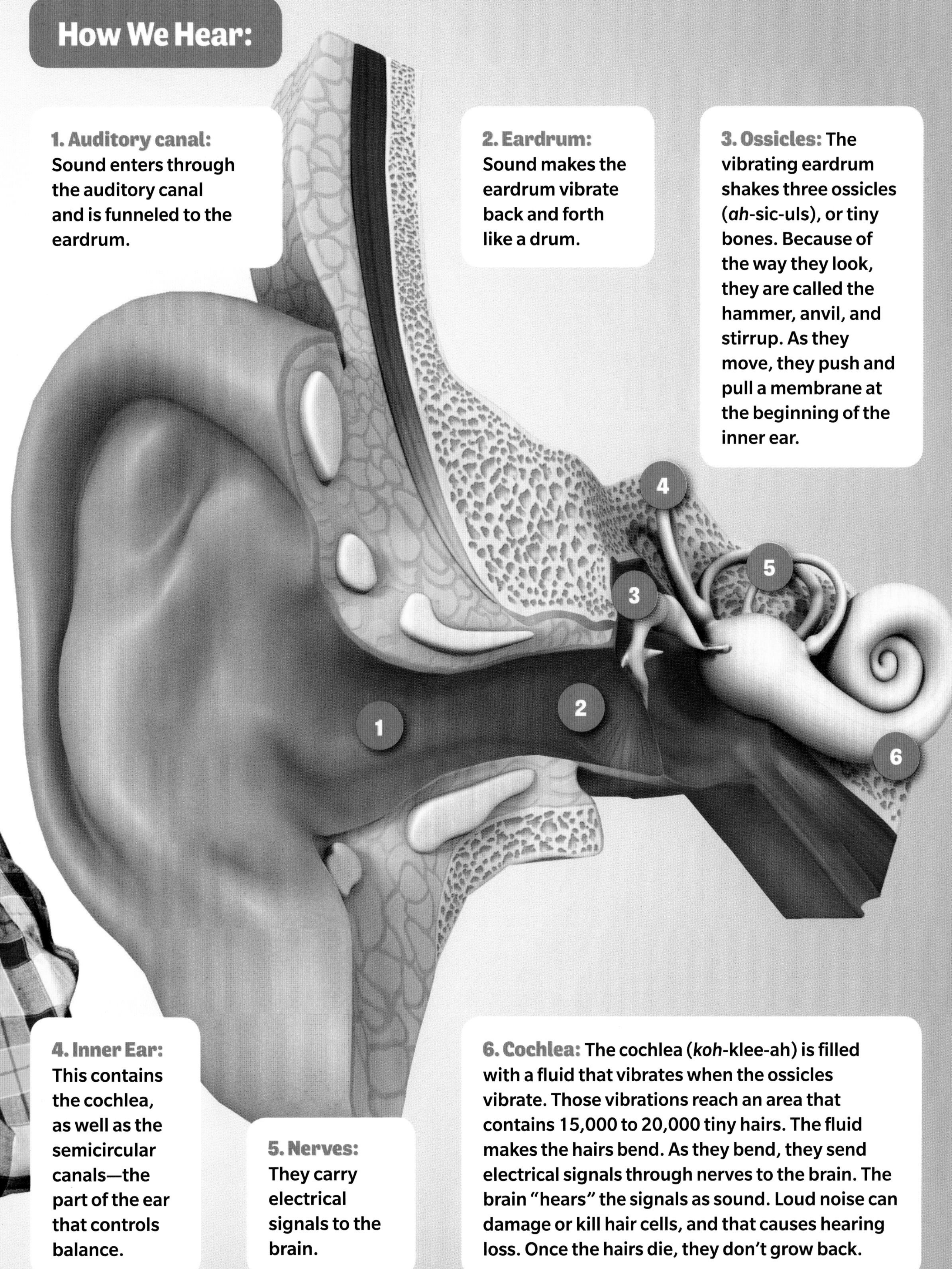

1. Auditory canal: Sound enters through the auditory canal and is funneled to the eardrum.

2. Eardrum: Sound makes the eardrum vibrate back and forth like a drum.

3. Ossicles: The vibrating eardrum shakes three ossicles (*ah*-sic-uls), or tiny bones. Because of the way they look, they are called the hammer, anvil, and stirrup. As they move, they push and pull a membrane at the beginning of the inner ear.

4. Inner Ear: This contains the cochlea, as well as the semicircular canals—the part of the ear that controls balance.

5. Nerves: They carry electrical signals to the brain.

6. Cochlea: The cochlea (*koh*-klee-ah) is filled with a fluid that vibrates when the ossicles vibrate. Those vibrations reach an area that contains 15,000 to 20,000 tiny hairs. The fluid makes the hairs bend. As they bend, they send electrical signals through nerves to the brain. The brain "hears" the signals as sound. Loud noise can damage or kill hair cells, and that causes hearing loss. Once the hairs die, they don't grow back.

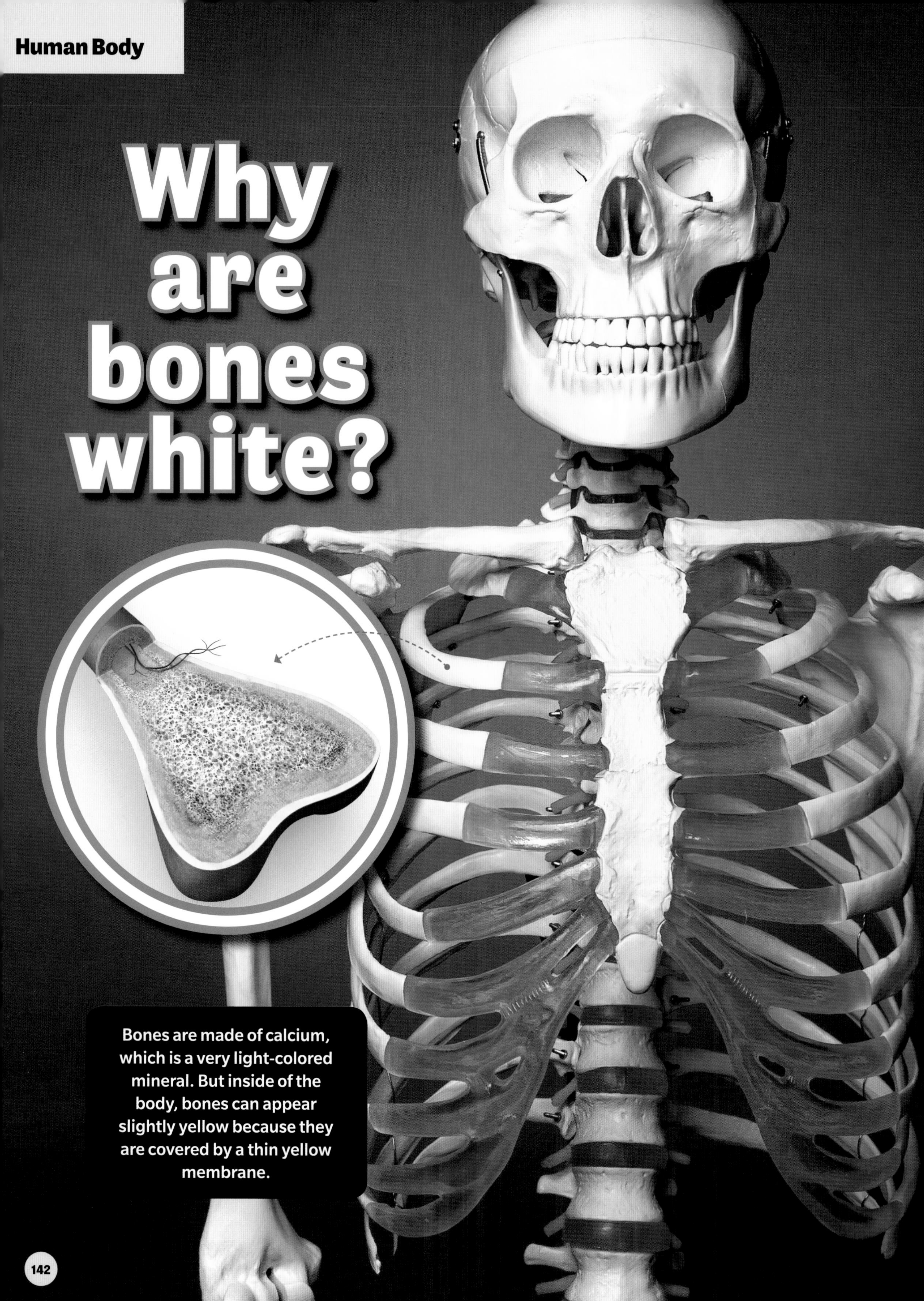

Why are bones white?

Bones are made of calcium, which is a very light-colored mineral. But inside of the body, bones can appear slightly yellow because they are covered by a thin yellow membrane.

Why are people ticklish?

When someone tickles you, they are stimulating the delicate nerve endings just under the skin. Some parts of our body are more ticklish than others. Feet are especially sensitive to tickling because feet have large nerve endings.

Why don't we laugh when we tickle ourselves?

Try it. Not much happens, right? You might think you would feel the same sensation as if someone else was tickling you. Not so. Scientists don't know why we can't tickle ourselves. Some suspect that the element of surprise has a lot to do with it. When we tickle ourselves, we have lost the surprise. Our brain—specifically the cerebellum—knows what is happening and that there's no reason to laugh.

How does the body fight germs?

Germs are all around us. Most are harmless, but a few can make us sick. When bacteria, viruses, and other microorganisms (tiny one-celled life forms) try to infect us, our immune system springs into action. To be immune is to be protected. The immune system has several ways to fight germs and keep us healthy. The first line of defense is our skin, which keeps out germs. The natural openings in the body, such as the mouth and eyes, produce chemicals to kill germs. If germs do get through our outer defenses, they are attacked by different types of white blood cells.

When we are infected, we feel sick: glands in the neck or armpits get swollen and tender, our temperature rises, skin that is cut might get red and sore. These are signs that our body is battling the germs.

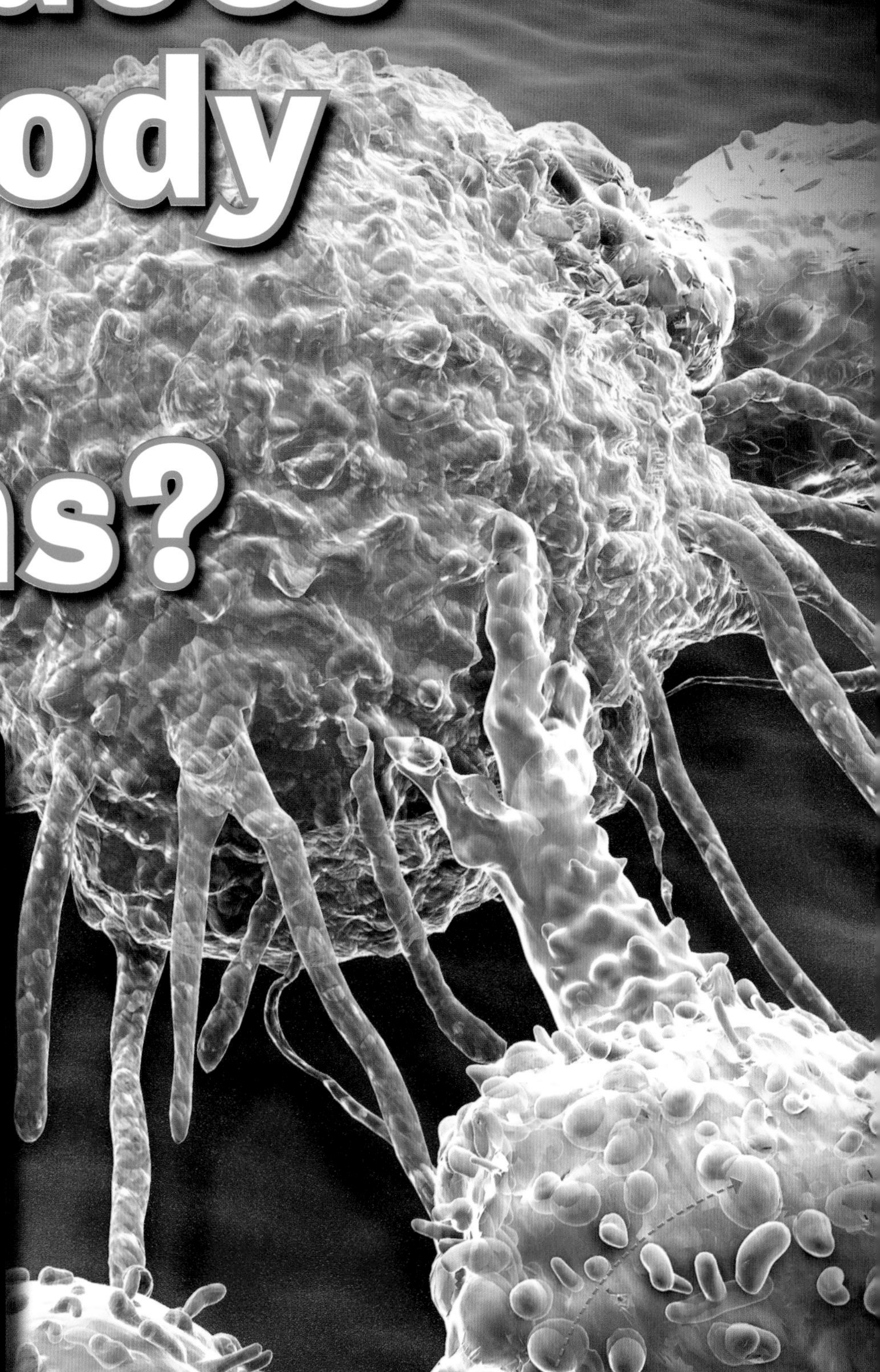

This computer-generated image shows a white blood cell called a **killer lymphocyte** (the ball on the right). As it travels through the body, it searches out and attacks cancer cells, as well as germs hiding in cells.

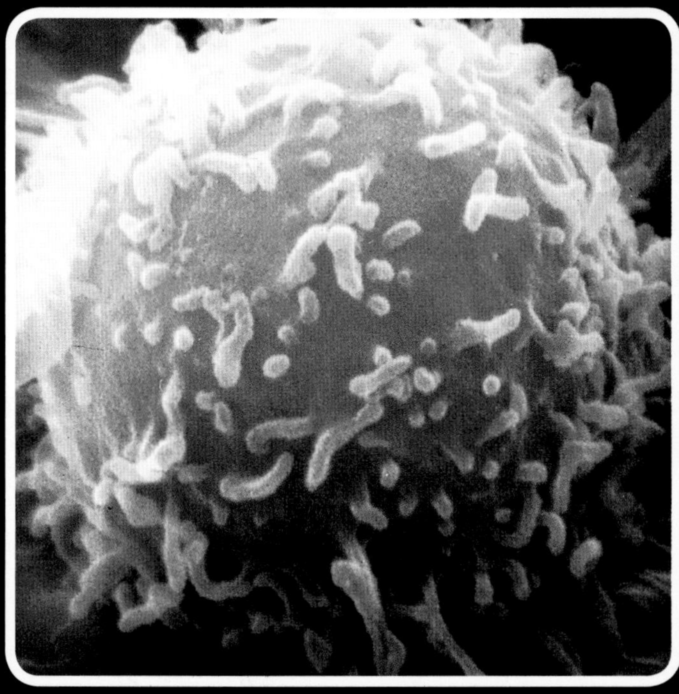

Shown here is a photo taken by an electron microscope of a special type of white blood cell called a **lymphocyte** (*lim*-foh-site). Some lymphocytes produce proteins called antibodies. The antibodies stick on germs, so other white blood cells know to kill them.

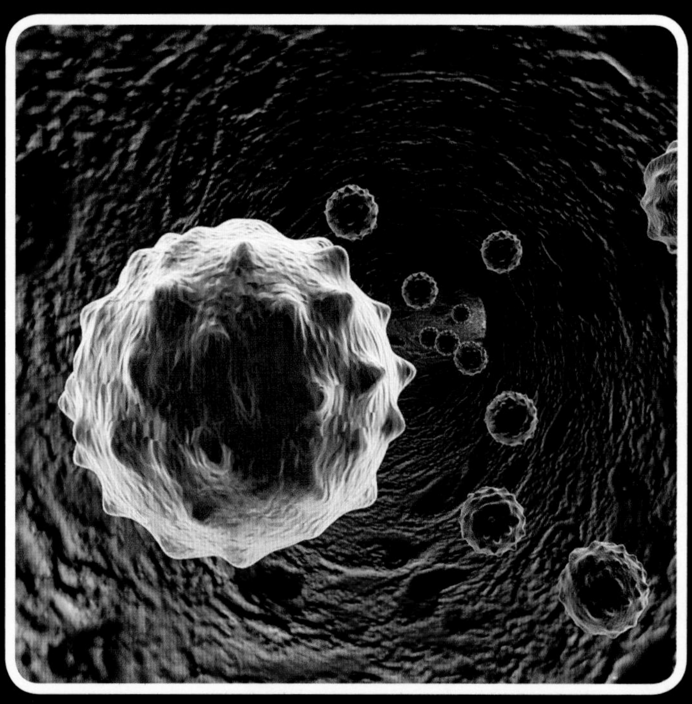

White blood cells, including macrophages (*mac*-roh-faj-ez), are in different organs and also travel through fluid in the lymph (limf) system and in the blood. They patrol the body looking for germs to swallow and kill. These cells are so small, they can only be seen through powerful microscopes.

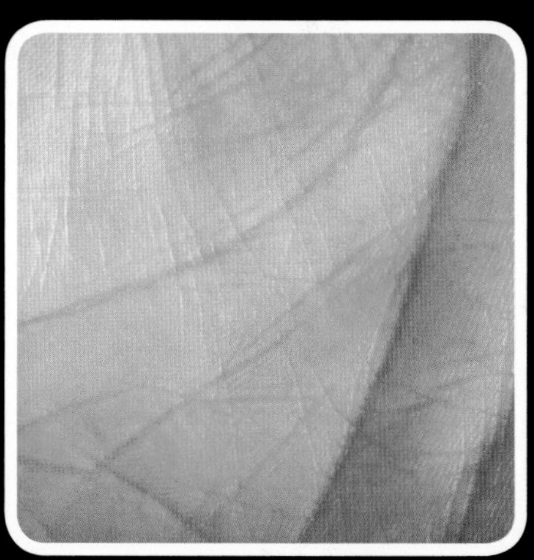

The surface of the **skin** is full of dead cells, which don't give germs a foothold. The skin also produces chemicals that can kill some bacteria.

Chemicals in saliva and in **tears** fight bacteria. **Stomach** acid kills bacteria.

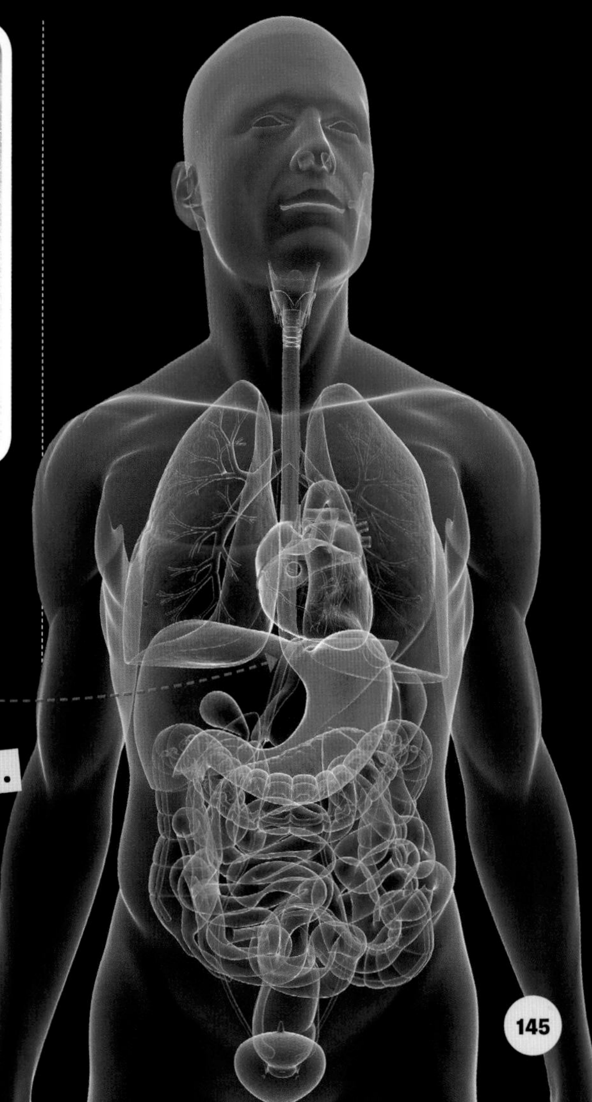

DID YOU KNOW? TOO MUCH STRESS OVER A LONG PERIOD OF TIME CAN WEAKEN THE IMMUNE SYSTEM. TALK OVER YOUR PROBLEMS WITH YOUR PARENTS OR TEACHERS. TO REDUCE STRESS, EXERCISE, ENJOY HOBBIES, READ FOR PLEASURE, OR PLAY WITH A PET.

Why do humans have fingerprints?

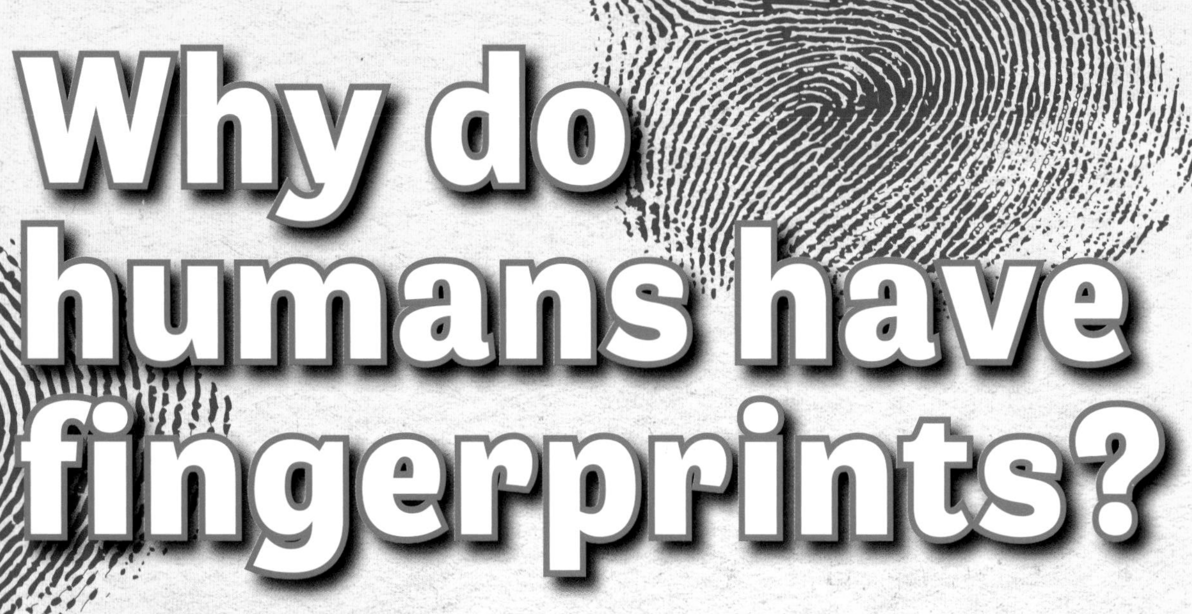

The series of lines, ridges, loops, and curves on the tips of your fingers are your fingerprints. Each person has a unique fingerprint. Genes play a part in the development of human fingerprints. However, when a baby is inside its mother's womb, it doesn't have any prints. Fingerprints develop as the baby presses against the inside of the womb. That's why identical twins have different fingerprints.

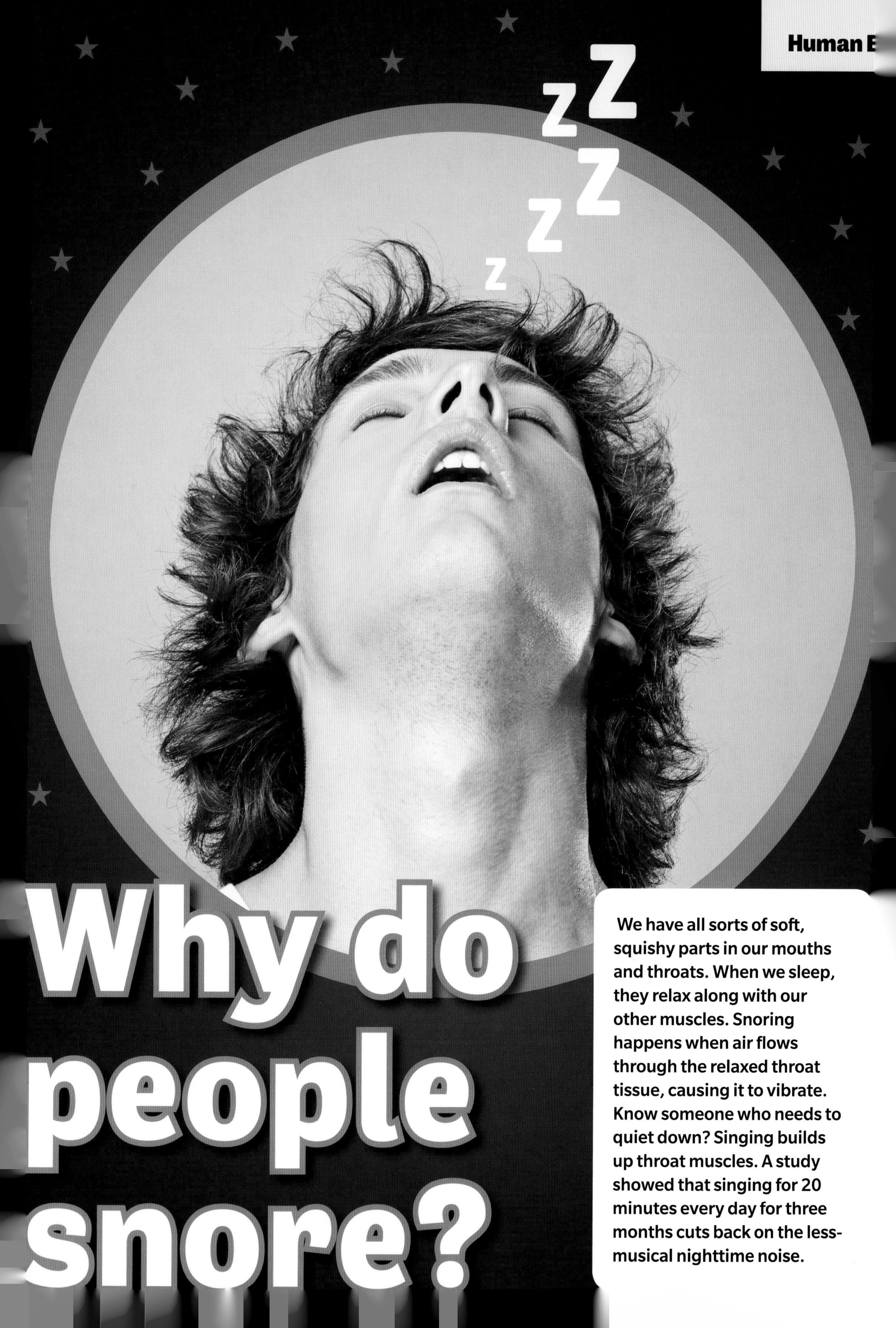

Why do people snore?

We have all sorts of soft, squishy parts in our mouths and throats. When we sleep, they relax along with our other muscles. Snoring happens when air flows through the relaxed throat tissue, causing it to vibrate. Know someone who needs to quiet down? Singing builds up throat muscles. A study showed that singing for 20 minutes every day for three months cuts back on the less-musical nighttime noise.

Transportation

Why are subs faster underwater than above it?

The streamline shape of a submarine lets it move more easily when it is entirely submerged in water. This wasn't always true. Older subs, such as those from World War II, did the opposite—they were designed to be faster on the surface than below it.

DID YOU KNOW? IN 1958, THE U.S. NUCLEAR SUBMARINE NAUTILUS BECAME THE FIRST TO COMPLETE A VOYAGE BENEATH THE ARCTIC ICE AT THE NORTH POLE.

Where is decorating trucks a popular pastime?

The roads of Pakistan are filled with trucks covered with colorful decorations. Truck art is a popular pastime. The owner usually pays for the work, but the driver or the artist often decides how the truck will be decorated. Although each truck is unique, there's a pattern to the decorations. The front often has a religious theme, with a taj, or wooden prow, built over the cab. Side panels are painted with landscapes and animals. The back panel is usually a large portrait surrounded by flowers or geometric patterns.

When was the first hot-air balloon launched?

Joseph Montgolfier wondered why smoke rose into the air. He also wondered if he could use whatever "force" was causing the smoke to rise to create some kind of flying machine. Working with his brother, Jacques-Etienne, Joseph hit on an idea: the hot-air balloon.

On September 19, 1783, Joseph and Etienne made history above the skies of Versailles, France. The king and queen were on hand to watch as the balloon took flight. It floated for about eight minutes and landed two miles away. The brothers didn't actually ride in the balloon's basket. Instead, the passengers were their pets: a duck, a sheep, and a rooster.

1783

Joseph and Etienne Montgolfier launch the first small hot-air balloon on June 4, 1783, over the village of Annonay, France. J.F. Pilâtre de Rozier and François Laurent become the first humans to fly. The pair drift over Paris on November 21, 1783, for about 20 minutes in a hot-air balloon designed by the Montgolfier brothers.

1785

A French balloonist, Jean-Pierre Blanchard, along with an American copilot, John Jeffries, become the first people to cross the English Channel in a hot-air balloon.

1892

The first weather balloons are built in France. The balloons carry instruments that measure barometric pressure, temperature, and humidity.

1907

Anderson Rubber Company in Akron, Ohio, makes the first hot-air balloons in the United States.

1982

An American truck driver named Larry Walters filled 45 weather balloons with helium. He hooked the balloons to a lawn chair and lifted off from his backyard in San Pedro, California. The ride took Walters more than 15,000 feet (4,572 meters) into the air.

1996

Balloonist Steve Fossett successfully crosses the Pacific Ocean flying solo in a helium balloon. He traveled from Korea to Canada in four days.

What is a hovercraft?

Imagine a vehicle that can travel on water, land, or ice. Does that make it a plane, a car, or a boat? It's the hovercraft, a vehicle that glides over land or sea on a cushion of air powered by air propellers or jet engines.

High-pressurized vents of air supplied by a powered fan underneath the craft press down on the surface, lifting the vehicle slightly. This constant air source is trapped by the vehicle's skirt, reducing friction and allowing it to move forward smoothly.

A Crafty Inventor

Christopher Cockerell, an English inventor, wanted to make the boat he was building go faster. He figured that a vehicle suspended on a cushion of air would quickly skim the water's surface. However, any fan he used would be larger than the boat. After trial and error, Cockerell realized that pressurized air around the rim of the boat could cause it to rise.

● The SR-N1

DID YOU KNOW? THE MILITARY USES HOVERCRAFT TO TRANSPORT TANKS AND OTHER HEAVY EQUIPMENT.

Out of Luck, Then Success

In 1952, Cockerell got busy designing and testing a model. He took it to the British government, thinking the armed forces could benefit from his invention. Although his idea was classified top secret, Cockerell didn't receive any money to develop the hovercraft further. He later complained, "The Navy said it was a plane not a boat; the Air Force said it was a boat not a plane; and the Army were 'plain not interested.'"

Five years later, the inventor built a full-scale model, the SR-N1. On July 25, 1959, the SR-N1 successfully crossed the English Channel in a little over two hours.

What will space travel look like?

Sixty years ago, space travel existed only in science-fiction novels. Today, astronauts have landed on the moon and lived in space for more than a year. What will the future hold for travel to the farthest reaches of our solar system?

Solar Sail

A spacecraft's weight is about 95 percent rocket fuel, making long-distance space flight extremely expensive. But what if there were a way to reduce the amount of fuel by harnessing the sun's energy to propel spacecraft once they reach space? Engineers are experimenting with solar-sail powered craft. Such a craft, made of lightweight, reflective material, would use sunlight as its power. Light particles bouncing off the reflective sail would push the craft forward at a faster and faster speed. A solar sail, however, would not be able to reach space on its own. It would need a traditional rocket to launch it. Once in space, though, the sail would have endless power from the sun and could travel indefinitely.

Space Tourism

Do you have $20 million to spare? That's the price for a one-week stay at the International Space Station. So far, at least five people have paid to experience life in space. Like astronauts, the tourists must prepare for their trip, spending several months training. In the years to come, more and more people will visit space. There is even talk of developing space hotels, where tourists could vacation and take spacewalks.

DID YOU KNOW? ENGINEERS ARE DEVELOPING AN ELEVATOR TO SEND PEOPLE INTO SPACE WITHO ROCKETS! THE SPACE ELEVATOR WOULD LET A SPACECRAFT CLIMB A CABLE INTO THE SKY.

How do bicycle gears make you go faster?

A bicycle is a great way to get around. It doesn't pollute, it's easy to ride, it's good exercise, and it's fun. One of the best things about a bike is that you can make the ride smoother with the press of a lever. What allows you to get in gear is, well, the gears.

A gear is a wheel with teeth that stick out. A bicycle has two sets of gears. One set is connected to the pedal, the other is attached to the rear wheel. A 3-speed bike has 3 gears, or "speeds." A mountain bike might have 24 gears. These gears let you change the distance the bike travels forward each time you turn the pedals. The higher the gear you put the bike in, the more distance you can travel with each turn of the pedals—and the faster you can go.

The **back gears** are turned by the chain. As the gears turn, so does the back wheel.

The **rear derailer** (derailleur) changes the back gears by moving the chain from gear to gear.

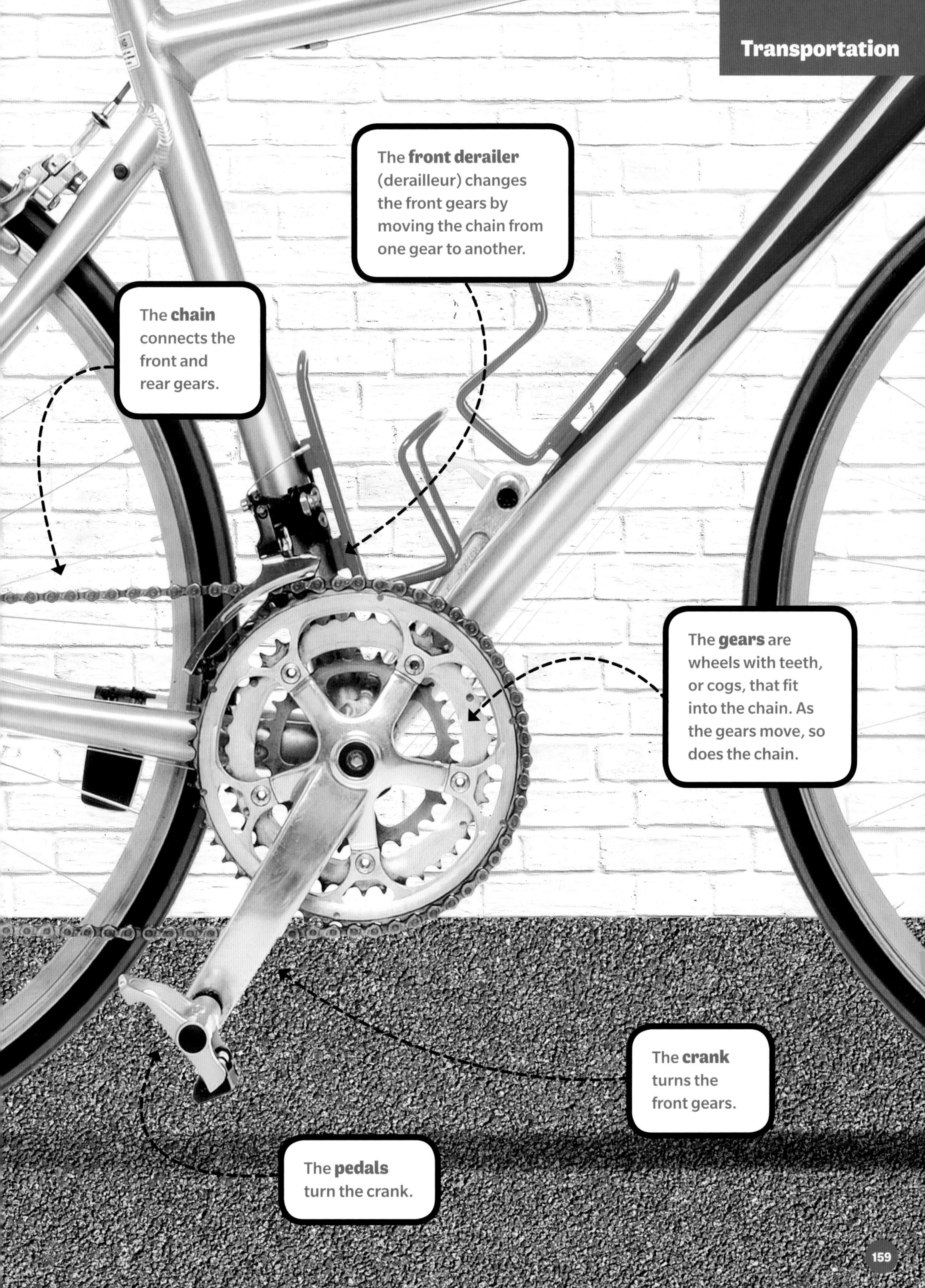
The **front derailer** (derailleur) changes the front gears by moving the chain from one gear to another.
The **chain** connects the front and rear gears.
The **gears** are wheels with teeth, or cogs, that fit into the chain. As the gears move, so does the chain.
The **crank** turns the front gears.
The **pedals** turn the crank.

Why do monster trucks have transparent floors?

Monster trucks are usually pickup trucks with super-large wheels. Their main tasks include looking cool, winning tug-of-war contests, and crushing cars. The cab might be as high as 15 feet (4.6m) off the ground, which means the driver can't see what's directly in front of the truck. The clear floor beneath the driver's feet makes it easier to see what's coming near—and under—its wheels.

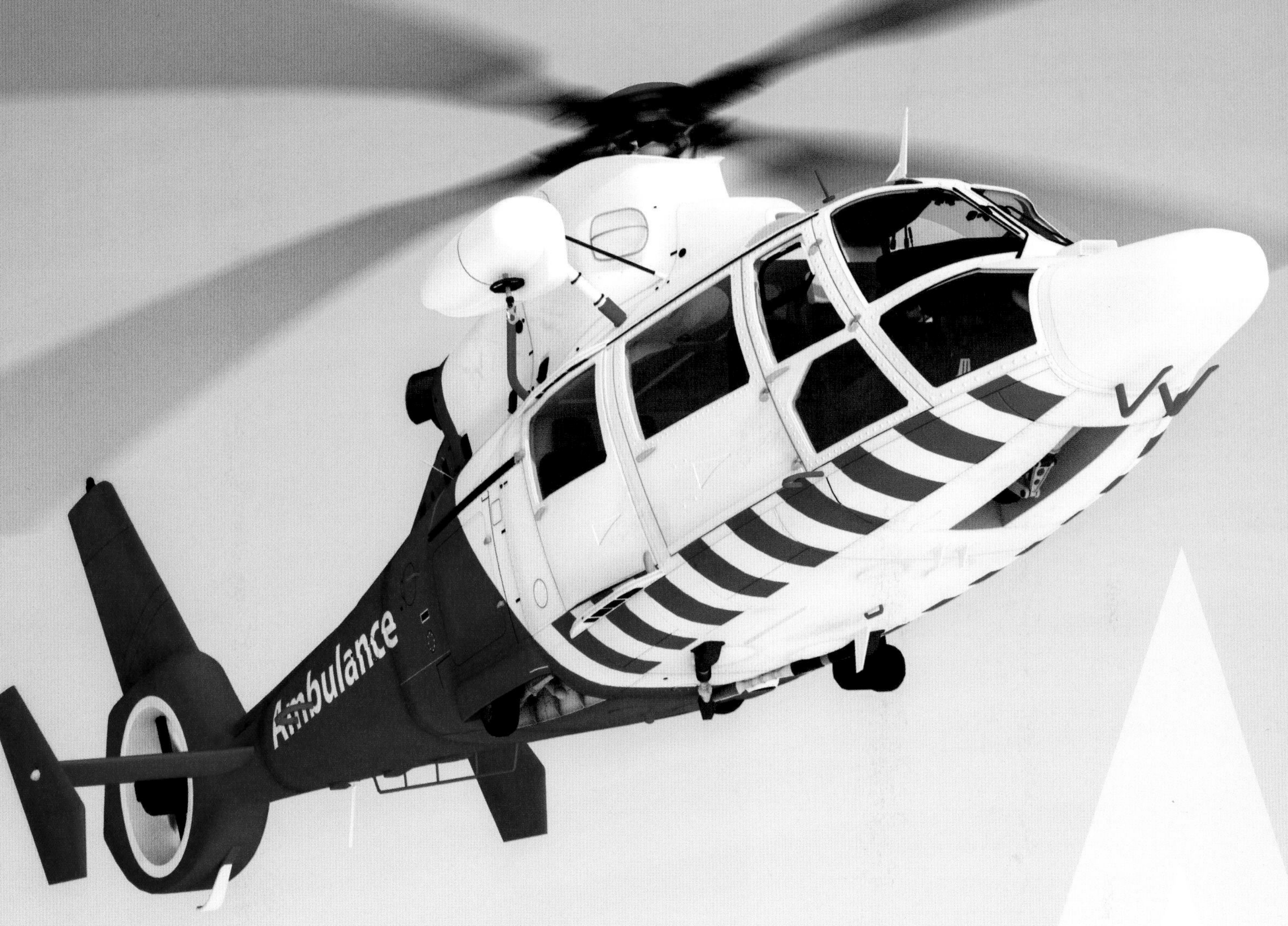

What do rotors on a helicpoter do?

On a helicopter, lift, or upward movement in the air, is produced by a copter's propellers called rotors. If a helicopter had only the large main rotor on top of the craft, it would spin in circles. A small rotor near the tail keeps the helicopter from whirling out of control. While airplanes can only fly horizontally, helicopters can move vertically and even hover in mid-air.

How does a maglev train work?

A levitating train floats in the air—but it's not a magic trick. Maglev is short for magnetic levitation, and maglev trains use the push and pull of magnetism to travel above the tracks. The opposite poles of a magnet attract each other. That attraction allows one kind of maglev train to levitate. The same poles of a magnet repel each other, which is why another kind of maglev train can float. With no friction from wheels to slow them down, these magnetic marvels can reach speeds of more than 300 miles per hour. Even the fastest American trains don't go faster than 80 miles per hour. Today, maglev trains are running full-time only in China. But maglev trains are being tested in Germany and Japan. They may one day come to the United States. When that happens, people who love riding trains will really be floating on air!

Electricity sent through wires in the guideway creates an electromagnetic field. The magnetism attracts or repels the maglev's magnets (depending on the type of train), lifting the cars as much as three inches.

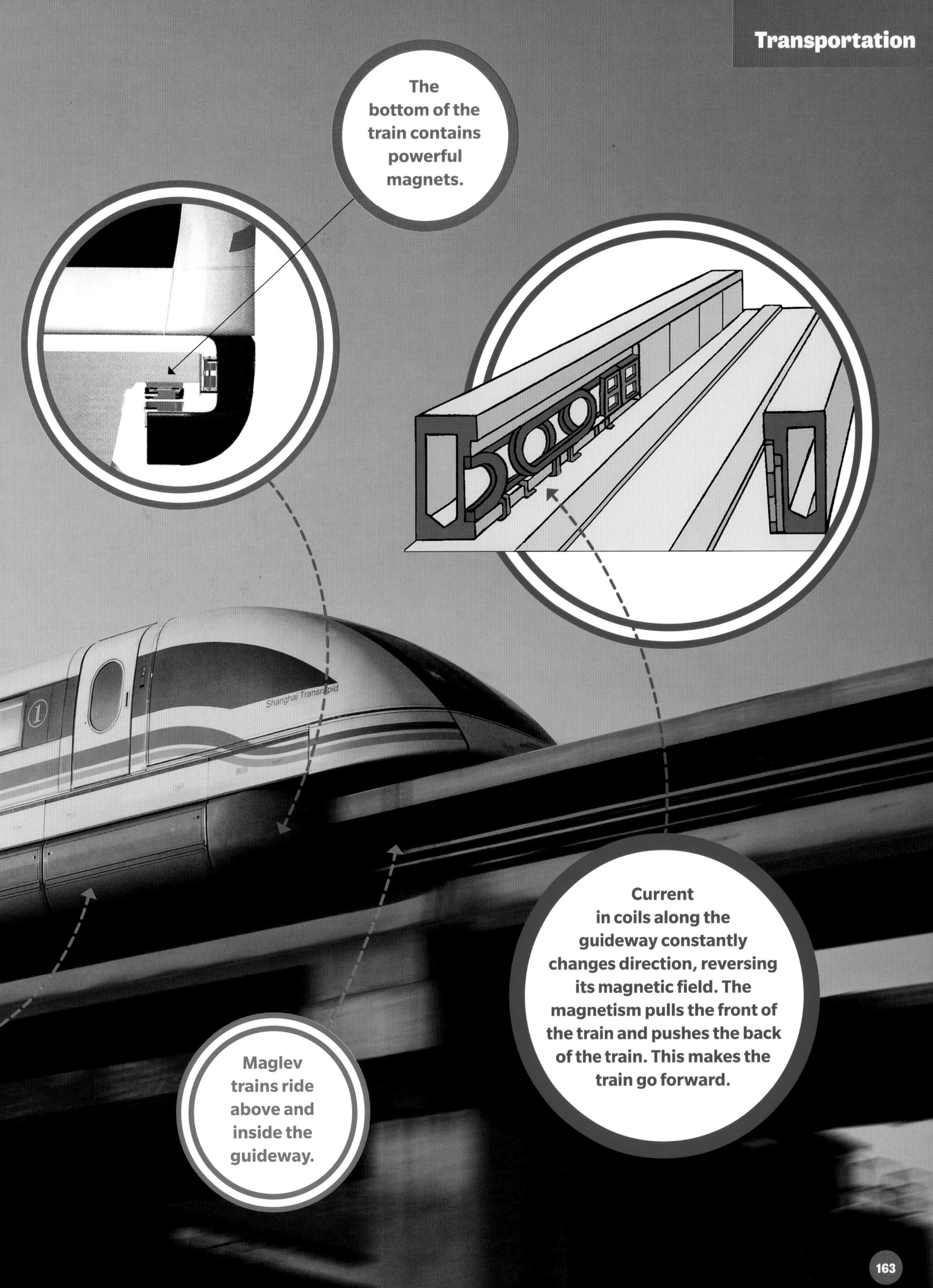
The bottom of the train contains powerful magnets.
Shanghai Transrapid
Current in coils along the guideway constantly changes direction, reversing its magnetic field. The magnetism pulls the front of the train and pushes the back of the train. This makes the train go forward.
Maglev trains ride above and inside the guideway.

When was the first motorcycle built?

Many people credit Gottlieb Daimler with inventing the first motorcycle in 1885. Daimler took a gasoline-powered engine and put it on a wooden-frame bicycle, known as the "bone crusher," because of its jarring ride. He placed two small wheels on the outside of the bike, and it became a motorcycle. Later, he went on to make automobiles.

The **seat** is designed to be as comfortable as possible for the driver.

Exhaust pipes release waste gas into the atmosphere after the gasoline burns.

The **drive chain** transfers power from the engine and gearbox to the rear wheel.

Foot pegs are located on either side of the bike.

The fuel tank holds the gasoline that powers the machine.

The throttle controls the power of the engine.

The front forks connect the bike frame to the front wheel.

The engine

Internal Combustion

At the heart of Daimler's bone crusher, and most other vehicles of the time, was the internal combustion engine, in which gasoline mixes with air. Inside the engine, a spark from a spark plug ignites the mixture, which causes the gasoline to explode. During the 1860s and 1870s, many people found innovative ways to turn these explosions into mechanical energy that could power machines and vehicles.

Two-Wheeled Drive

In 1892, the Millet became the first successful two-wheeled motorbike. Previous two-wheeled designs had failed because the bikes tipped over. This bike, however, stayed upright despite the five-cylinder rotary engine in the hub of its rear wheel.

When did the first commercial airliner take flight?

On January 1, 1914, Antony H. Jannus sat behind the controls of an airboat owned by the St. Petersburg-Tampa Airboat Line. He fired up the engines and took off across Tampa Bay in Florida. It was the world's first winged airliner and the world's first airline flight.

This plane was built with wood, cloth, and wire. On board was Abram C. Pheil, the first-ever airline passenger. He sat on a small wooden seat near the pilot and wore a raincoat so he would not get wet. Jannus unexpectedly had to land in the water to fix the sputtering engine. He took off again and landed safely on the Hillsborough River. A crowd of 3,500 people greeted Jannus and Pheil.

● The first commercial flight was in a Benoist flying boat.

DID YOU KNOW? THE REGULAR PRICE OF THE TICKET WAS $5 FOR THE 22-MINUTE TRIP FROM ST. PETERSBURG TO TAMPA. BUT ABRAM C. PHEIL PAID $400 FOR HIS TICKET, WHICH WAS SOLD AT AUCTION TO THE HIGHEST BIDDER.

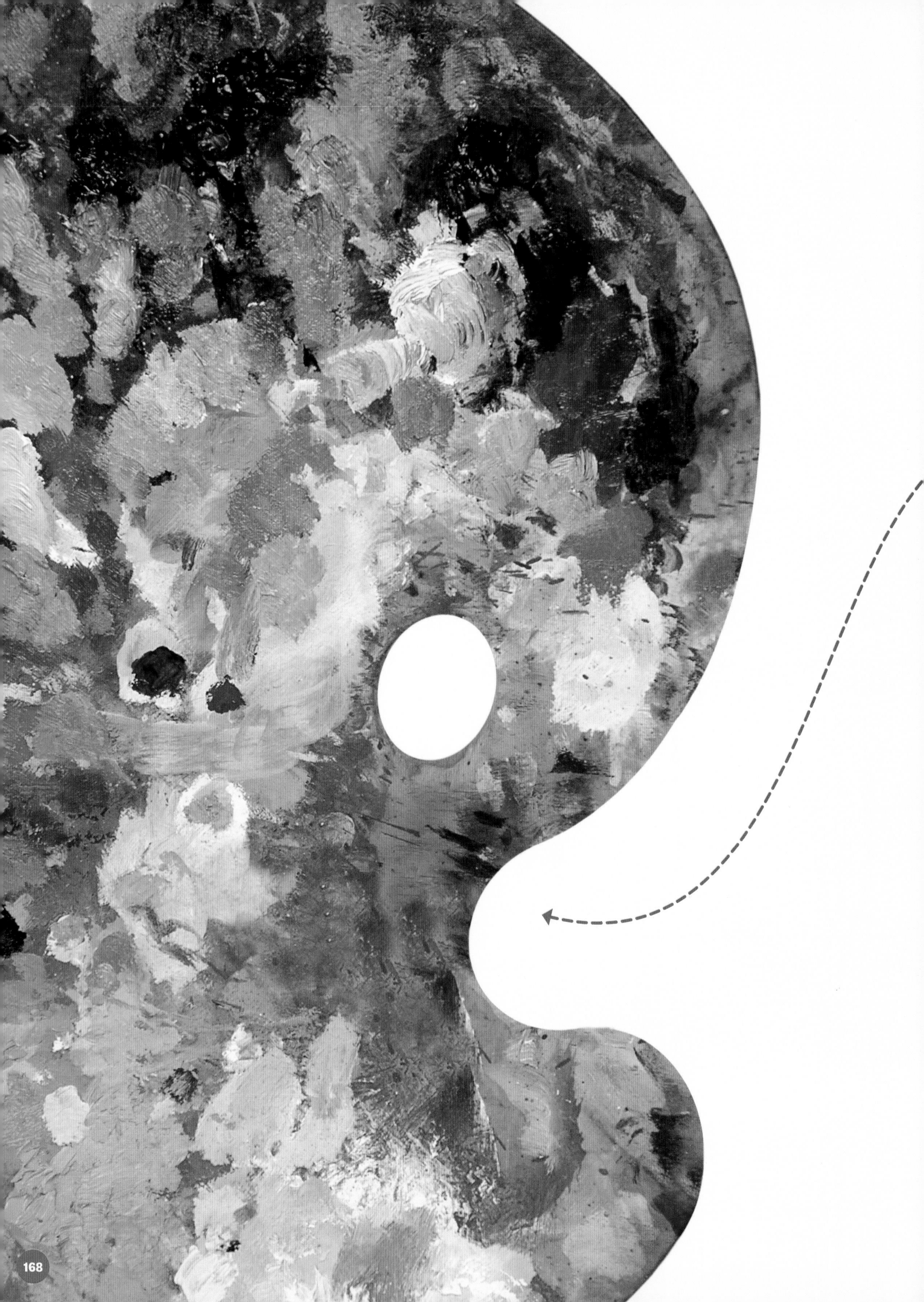

Arts

Where did an artist spend four years painting a ceiling?

Although a book and movie portray Michelangelo Buonarotti as lying on his back to paint the ceiling of the Sistine Chapel in Vatican City, it just wasn't so. He did, however, spend four years standing on ledges and platforms 65 feet high and bending his head back to paint. In a funny poem, Michelangelo described his discomfort: "My beard toward Heaven, I feel the back of my brain upon my neck . . . In front of me my skin is being stretched while it folds up behind and forms a knot."

Michelangelo used the fresco technique, applying paint to the plaster of the ceiling while it was still wet. Although he probably used assistants to make the plaster and grind and mix the colors, Michelangelo did all the painting. More than 400 life-size figures illustrate scenes from the Bible. Despite the pain Michelangelo suffered, he created a masterpiece that has astonished visitors for more than 500 years.

● **It took Michelangelo (right) four years to paint the ceiling of the Sistine Chapel in Vatican City.**

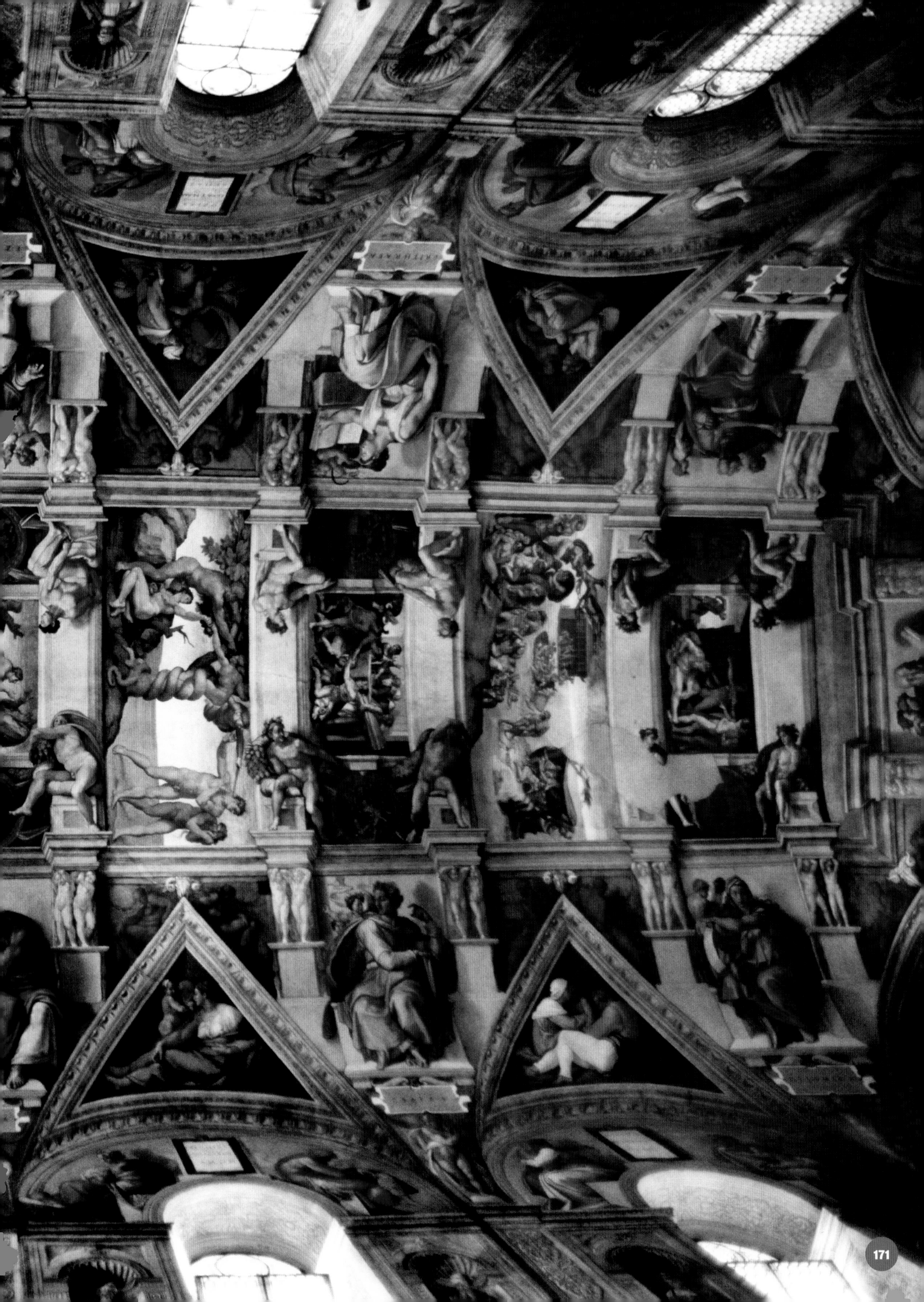

Why are there stars on the sidewalk in Hollywood?

Some cities give their heroes statues. In the Hollywood section of Los Angeles, California, famous entertainers are given metal-and-stone stars on the sidewalks. There are about 2,500 stars on the Hollywood Walk of Fame. Each star lists the entertainer's name and the way he or she became famous, such as through movies, TV, radio, music, or theater.

THE SIMPSONS

Why are the Academy Awards called the Oscars?

Officially, the Academy of Motion Picture Arts and Sciences calls their annual award the "Academy Award of Merit." But the gold statues have been known as Oscars since 1934. One story says that an Academy librarian thought the statue looked like her Uncle Oscar. Another story credits newspaperman Sidney Skolsky with making up the nickname.

● Actresses Jennifer Lawrence and Anne Hathaway celebrate their Oscar wins in 2013.

Where is the world's most visited museum?

DID YOU KNOW? THE MONA LISA—PAINTED BY LEONARDO DA VINCI IN THE EARLY 16TH CENTURY—CAN BE FOUND IN THE LOUVRE AND IS ONE OF THE MOST FAMOUS PAINTINGS IN THE WORLD.

Every year, almost nine million people come from all over the world to visit the Louvre (*lou*-vruh) in Paris, France. When the first building went up more than 800 years ago, however, it wasn't a museum but a fortress. When the city grew up around it, the fortress, no longer used for defense, was transformed into a palace for the king.

In the 1600s, the royal family moved to a new palace just outside Paris. The old palace was then used for exhibits. Finally, on August 10, 1793, the Louvre opened as a museum. Admission was free. Artists could visit anytime, but the public was only allowed in on weekends. The works on display were mostly paintings from the collections of the king and other noble families. The Louvre has been growing ever since.

Today, the museum's collection includes about 380,000 works of art, with about 35,000 on display. Among the most famous are the *Law Code of Hammurabi, King of Babylon*; the *Winged Victory of Samothrace*; the *Venus de Milo*; and Leonardo da Vinci's *Mona Lisa*.

Where did J.K. Rowling get the name Potter?

● Author J.K. Rowling created the boy wizard Harry Potter.

A brother and sister who were children in author J.K. Rowling's neighborhood were named Potter. Rowling has said that she liked their name better than hers because other kids made fun of her name.

● Theodor Seuss Geisel created memorable characters like the Cat in the Hat.

Who is the "real" Dr. Seuss?

You've probably read some books written by Dr. Seuss. Dr. Seuss's characters have unusual names, like Horton, the Cat in the Hat, Sam I Am, and the Grinch. But what about the author's name? Dr. Seuss isn't the real name of the writer of all those books. It is Theodor Seuss Geisel. He was not a real doctor. He added Dr. to his name because his father wanted Theodor to earn a doctorate degree as a college professor. More than 200 million Dr. Seuss books have been sold. They've been translated into 15 languages. In addition, his works have been made into television specials, movies, and a Broadway play.

What was the Jazz age?

DID YOU KNOW? JAZZ GOT ITS START IN THE 1880s IN NEW ORLEANS, LOUISIANA. FUNERAL BANDS PLAYING BRASSY MUSIC WOULD MARCH BEHIND HEARSES. BY THE 1920S, JAZZ BECAME KNOWN THROUGHOUT THE UNITED STATES.

For Americans, the 1920s were a swinging time. World War I had recently ended, and people were making more money than ever before. They bought cars, radios, and new-fangled appliances, such as refrigerators, washing machines, and vacuum cleaners. They were out to enjoy life to the fullest. People poured into movie theaters, where they watched silent movies and, starting in 1927, the first talkies. They visited dance halls, swinging their arms and knocking their knees together as they danced the Charleston. They went to clubs to hear jazz, music that combined the beats of Africa with the instruments of Europe.

This exciting period came to be known as the Jazz Age. The good times lasted until 1929, when the stock market crashed and plunged the nation into the Great Depression, a time of very high unemployment.

The Flap Over Flappers

The 1920s brought big changes for women. Many wore shorter skirts, cut their long hair, and put on lipstick and make up. Called "flappers," they did the kind of things that once only men did, such as drive cars. Many people, especially those who were older, disapproved of flappers' dress and behavior. And in 1929, Florida even tried to prohibit people in the state from using the word!

Why do people call Broadway the Great White Way?

They say the lights are bright on Broadway–so bright that they call New York City's theater district the Great White Way. At the beginning of the 20th century, 16 theatres were on Broadway itself and many others were located near the famous avenue. The fronts of all these theatres blazed with lights to call attention to the plays.

Why are Impressionist painters so important?

For thousands of years, the goal of most artists was to make their pictures look as realistic as possible. But in the late 1800s, a group of artists invented a new approach. They painted their impressions of scenes, rather than exact pictures of what they saw. Impressionism focuses on subtle changes in color brought about by light. At the time, the work of French Impressionist painters like Claude Monet, Edgar Degas, and Pierre-Auguste Renoir was rejected, but now it ranks among the world's most valuable art.

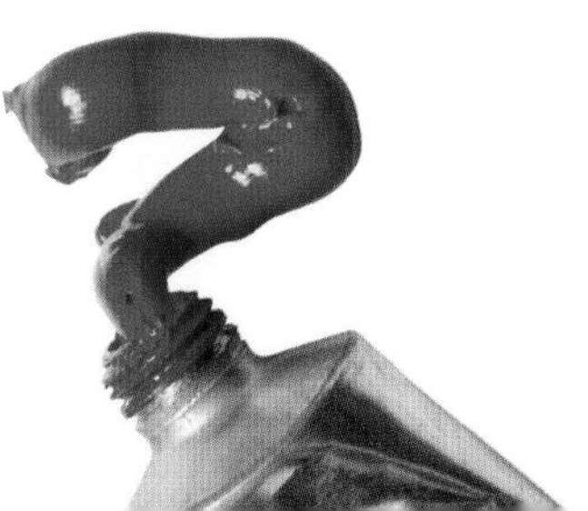

What is a geodesic dome?

A geodesic dome is hard to miss. The structure is shaped like a partial sphere and it's made up of interlocking pyramid shapes called tetrahedrons. Lightweight, yet extremely strong and stable, the geodesic dome uses less material to cover more space than any other structure ever built.

● Buckminster Fuller stands in front of one of his geodesic domes.

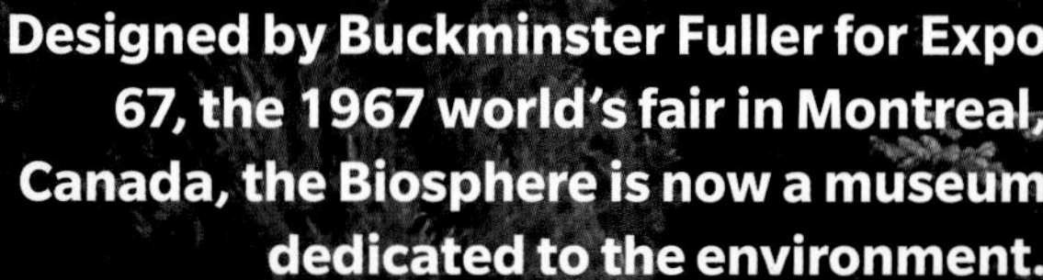

On Display
Designed by Buckminster Fuller for Expo 67, the 1967 world's fair in Montreal, Canada, the Biosphere is now a museum dedicated to the environment.

A Man Ahead of His Time

The man who patented the geodesic dome was Buckminster Fuller, an American engineer and inventor. In the 1950s, he designed the geodesic dome in an effort to provide low-cost housing. While the domes never caught on as places to live, they are used as airplane hangars, greenhouses, observatories, theaters, sports arenas, and planetariums.

Play Ball!

Located in Toronto, Canada, the SkyDome, home to the Toronto Blue Jays, is a geodesic dome with a retractable roof. On sunny days, the roof can open completely so players and fans can enjoy the weather. When it rains or snows, the roof closes.

Disney Magic

A complete sphere, Spaceship Earth is more a globe than a dome. Still, the Disney World attraction is perhaps the most famous geodesic dome ever built. It towers 180 feet high and can easily be seen for miles around.

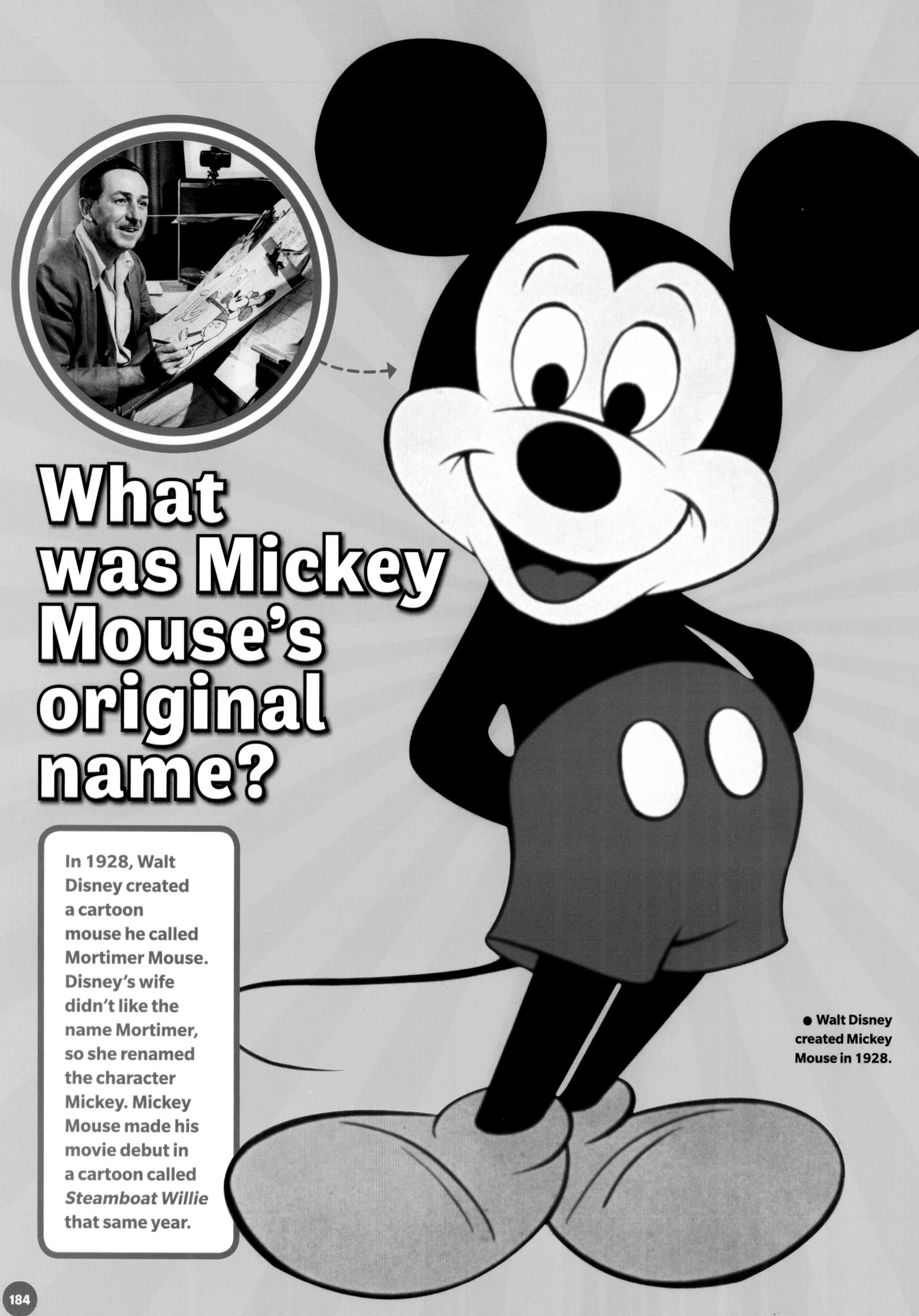

What was Mickey Mouse's original name?

In 1928, Walt Disney created a cartoon mouse he called Mortimer Mouse. Disney's wife didn't like the name Mortimer, so she renamed the character Mickey. Mickey Mouse made his movie debut in a cartoon called *Steamboat Willie* that same year.

● Walt Disney created Mickey Mouse in 1928.

● Elvis Presley is known as the King of Rock 'n' Roll.

What was the first rock 'n' roll song?

No one person invented rock 'n' roll. That's why it's not easy to figure out what was the first rock 'n' roll song. Although you may not know some of these first rock musicians, many fans believe that Bill Haley's *Rock Around the Clock* (1954) was the first rock 'n' roll record. Many others believe it was Elvis Presley's *That's All Right Mama* (1954). Others say a song called *Rocket 88* (1951) by Jackie Brenston was the granddaddy of them all.

acid rain precipitation that has high acidity because of being mixed with pollutants

Antarctica the ice-covered continent around the South Pole

antibiotic a medicine that kills bacteria

antibodies proteins in the body that fight off disease and infection

arachnophobia a fear of spiders

Arctic the area around the North Pole

asteroids rocks, some the size of small planets, that orbit between Mars and Jupiter

atmosphere the envelope of gases around the Earth

bacteria microscopic single-celled organisms found in water, air, and soil

camanchaca heavy fog that forms in the Atacama Desert and moves inland

canyon a deep valley with steep sides, often formed by a river

caravansaries large stone buildings that served as inns

cavity a hole formed in a tooth by decay

cells the basic structure of all living things; in a beehive, six-sided structures made of beeswax that store food and house growing bees

centrifugal force the force directed away from the center of a revolving body

cerebellum back part of the brain that controls balance and the use of muscles

civil rights the rights that every person should have regardless of his or her race or gender

cochlea the part of the inner ear that carries information about sound to the brain

comet a large chunk of rock surrounded by frozen gas and ice that orbits the sun

communicate to express information or ideas

constellation a group of stars that seem to form a pattern in the sky

decibel a unit used to measure loudness

derailer (derailleur) a device on a bicycle that shifts gears by moving a chain from one gear wheel to another

DNA the chemical that carries the structure for every living thing

empire a group of countries or regions that are controlled by one ruler

environment the external surroundings in which a plant or animal lives

fossil part of a plant or animal from the distant past that has been preserved in Earth's crust

friction the force that causes a moving object to slow down when it is touching another object

Glossary

gear a wheel with teeth that turns another wheel with teeth, so the motion of one controls the speed of the other

gene a part of a cell that controls or influences the appearance of a living thing

geothermal energy heat produced inside Earth

gladiator a man in ancient Rome who fought against another man or animal for public entertainment

gland a cell or group of cells that produce a substance that a body uses or gets rid of

Global Positioning System (GPS) a satellite navigation system that is used to determine an exact location on Earth

global warming an increase in the average temperature of the Earth

gravity the force of attraction between two objects

greenhouse gas a gas, such as carbon dioxide and methane, that contributes to global warming

hive a structure that houses a colony of bees

honeycomb a group of cells made of beeswax in a beehive

hormone a natural substance in the body that influences the way the body grows or develops

immune system cells, proteins, and tissue that protect the body from infection and disease

Impressionism an important art movement in which artists painted their impressions of what they saw rather than an exact picture

infection the invasion of the body by a microorganism, such as a virus, that causes disease

internal combustion engine the type of engine used in most vehicles in which the fuel is burned within engine cylinders

jazz a type of music with African-American roots developed in the 20th century and characterized by improvisation and intricate rhythms

Komodo dragon a large species of lizard found in Indonesia

krill small, shrimplike sea creatures

lichen a type of small plant that grows on rocks and walls

lymph system the tissues and organs that produce and carry cells that fight infections

lysozyme a chemical in tears that fights germs

magnetic field the area affected by the pull and push of a magnet or an object such as the sun or Earth that produces magnetism

magnetism the attracting of certain metals

magnetron a vacuum tube used to generate microwaves

mammal a warm-blooded animal with a backbone that has hair or fur and feeds milk to their young

masterpiece a work done with great skill

membrane a layer of tissue that is part of a plant or an animal's body

meteorite a mass of stone or metal that has fallen from space

meteorologist a scientist who studies the climate and weather

microchip an integrated circuit

microwave electromagnetic radiation, similar to radio waves, that is used in microwave ovens to cook food

molecule the smallest part of a substance, made up of one or more atoms

mucus a thick fluid that coats and protects the nose, throat, lungs, and other areas of the body

muscle a body tissue that produces movement

neuron a cell that carries messages between the brain and other parts of the body

orbit the path one body takes around another, such as the path of the Earth around the sun

ossicle a tiny bone

photon a tiny particle of light

potential energy stored energy in an object

predator an animal that kills other animals for food

processor a chip that processes the basic instructions that drive a computer

propeller spinning blades that make a boat, submarine, or airplane move

prototypes the first models on which later models are developed or based

pyramid a massive monument with a rectangular base and four triangular faces

radiation the process in which energy is emitted as particles or waves

rain forest a dense forest that grows in warm or tropical regions where it rains heavily throughout the year

satellite a machine that is sent into space and that moves around the earth, moon, sun, or a planet

space probe an unmanned spacecraft designed to explore the solar system and send information back to Earth

species a group of similar organisms

spoilers the wings in the rear of a car that help reduce lift when it travels at high speeds

submarine a ship that operates underwater

tectonic plate the slabs of rock that make up the surface of the Earth

tornado a dark, funnel-shaped cloud made of fast-spinning air

transformer a device that transfers electrical energy from one circuit to another

transistor an electronic device that controls the flow of an electric current and is used as an amplifier or switch

transmit to send out a signal

wind turbine a machine that turns the power of the wind into electrical energy

Index

A

Photo Credits

Back Cover: Christian Petersen/Getty Images; sevenke/Shutterstock; solarseven/Shutterstock; Racheal Grazias/Shutterstock; Andrey Kuzmin/Shutterstock
Page 3: sevenke/Shutterstock
Pages 4–5: Sergey Uryadnikov/Shutterstock; Celso Diniz/Shutterstock; R-O-M-A/Shutterstock; Chones/Shutterstock; AGIF/Shutterstock; Timothy Hodgkinson/Shutterstock; Dundanim/Shutterstock; Gorich/Shutterstock; 2bears/Shutterstock; R. Gino Santa Maria/Shutterstock
Page 6: Sergey Uryadnikov/Shutterstock
Page 8: Retales Botijero/Getty Images
Page 9: Watt Jim/Getty Images
Pages 10–11: Mark Bridger/Shutterstock
Page 12: OHishiapply/Shutterstock; sevenke/Shutterstock; Joel Sartore/Getty Images
Page 13: takayuki/Shutterstock; Talvi/Shutterstock; Ben Cranke/Getty Images
Page 14: Mint Images/Art Wolfe/Getty Images
Page 15: David Tipling/Getty Images; Sylvain Cordier/Getty Images; Eastcott Momatiuk/Getty Images; National Geographic/Getty Images
Page 16: David Haring/DUPC/Getty Images (2); Mark Carwardine/Getty Images
Page 17: Pyty/Shutterstock
Page 18: Elenarts/Shutterstock
Page 19: O. Louis Mazzatenta/National Geographic/Getty Images; Ondrej Prosicky/Shutterstock
Page 20: Shaiith/Shutterstock
Page 21: Beehive Illustration by Lon Tweeten and Ed Gabel for TIME
Page 22: DreamBig/Shutterstock
Page 23: Dan Kosmayer/Shutterstock
Page 24: Joseph Nettis/Getty Images
Page 25: Luis Robayo/AFP/Getty Images
Page 26: Celso Diniz/Shutterstock
Pages 28–29: 3Dsculptor/Shutterstock; NASA/Getty Images; Science Source/Getty Images; Adastra/Image Bank/Getty Images/ NASA/Bill Ingalls; Alan Freed/Shutterstock
Page 30: EpicStockMedia/Shutterstock
Page 31: AFP/Getty Images; NASA Images
Pages 32–33: NASA (2)
Page 34: NASA/The LIFE Picture Collection/Getty Images
Page 35: Festa/Shutterstock
Pages 36–37: NASA (4)
Pages 38–39: NASA (6)
Page 40: NASA (2)
Page 41: Everett Historical/Shutterstock
Pages 42–43: R-O-M-A/Shutterstock
Pages 44–45: Martin Bisof/Shutterstock; Fotos593/Shutterstock
Page 46: Volodymyr Martyniuk/Shutterstock
Page 47: Imagno/Getty Images; Michael Schmeling/Getty Images; caesart/Shutterstock
Page 48: Peter Bernik/Shutterstock; INTERPHOTO/Alamy/IndiaPicture
Page 49: Veronika Galkina/Shutterstock
Page 50: Fotosearch/Getty Images; WitthayaP/Shutterstock
Page 51: UIG/Getty Images; Aksenenko Olga/Shutterstock
Page 52: Francis Miller/The LIFE Picture Collection/Getty Images
Page 53: f9photos/Shutterstock
Pages 54–57: Courtesy of National Park Service, U.S. Department of the Interior (8)
Page 58: Stuart Keasley/Robert Harding World Imagery/Getty Images; Kaspri/Shutterstock
Page 59: Time Life Pictures/Getty Images
Pages 60–61: Chones/Shutterstock
Pages 62–63: zhu difeng/Shutterstock; andrea crisante/Shutterstock; stefan11/Shutterstock
Page 64: javarman/Shutterstock; Andrey Popov/Shutterstock; Snowbelle/Shutterstock
Page 65: Igor Kovalchuk/Shutterstock; Maxx-Studio/Shutterstock; Inozemtsev Konstantin/Shutterstock
Page 66: Racheal Grazias/Shutterstock
Page 67: Neil Lang/Shutterstock; Margie Hurwich/Shutterstock; Christian Bertrand/ Shutterstock; StacieStauffSmith Photos/Shutterstock; SIHASAKPRACHUM/Shutterstock
Pages 68–69: solarseven/Shutterstock; Vitoriano Junior/Shutterstock
Pages 70–71: istockphoto.com
Page 72: Cardaf/Shutterstock
Page 73: Ase/Shutterstock; Jon Schulte/Getty Images; Kingwu/Getty Images; photokup/Shutterstock; Stephen Mulcahey/Shutterstock; Rhonda Roth/Shutterstock
Page 74: Richard Packwood/Oxford Scientific/Getty Images; 3Kletr/Shutterstock
Page 75: vitstudio/Shutterstock
Pages 76–77: AGIF/Shutterstock
Pages 78–79: John W. McDonough/Sports Illustrated (6)
Page 80: Bob Thomas/Popperfoto/Getty Images (2)
Page 81: Richard Mackson for Sports Illustrated
Pages 82–83: Marcel Jancovic/Shutterstock; fzd.it/Shutterstock
Page 84: HodagMedia/Shutterstock; bioraven/Shutterstock
Page 85: David E. Klutho/Sports Illustrated; Pictorial Parade/Archive Photos/Getty Images
Pages 86–87: Christian Petersen/Getty Images; A. Ricardo/Shutterstock; Al Messerschmidt/Getty Images
Pages 88–89: Al Tielemans /Sports Illustrated (5); David Lee/Shutterstock
Page 90: James Flores/Getty Images
Page 91: SCOTTCHAN/Shutterstock
Page 92: Timothy Hodgkinson/Shutterstock
Pages 94–95: INTERFOTO/ Alamy; Apic/Getty Images; Shawn Hempel/Shutterstock; Hellen Sergeyeva/Shutterstock
Pages 96–97: Hellen Sergeyeva/Shutterstock; Ted Streshinsky/The LIFE Images Collection/Getty Images; Texas Instruments (2)
Pages 98–99: meunierd/Shutterstock; Djedi team (2)
Page 100: Jens Schlueter/Getty Images News
Page 101: Berka7/Shutterstock; Photolibrary/North Wind Pictures
Pages 102–103: Mahathir Mohd Yasin/Shutterstock; GooDween123/Shutterstock; Ildi Papp/Shutterstock; janecocoa/Shutterstock; Viktor1/Shutterstock
Pages 104–105: The LEGO Group; Bloomberg/Getty Images; Maryutin Maxim/Shutterstock; seewhatmitchsee/Shutterstock
Page 106: Fox Photos/Getty Images
Page 107: Refat/Shutterstock; Nagel Photography/Shutterstock; Mike Flippo/Shutterstock; stockphoto-graf/Shutterstock; ARENA Creative/Shutterstock; Giulio Fornasar/Shutterstock; Galushko Sergey/Shutterstock
Page 108: anigoweb/Shutterstock; Zern Liew/Shutterstock
Page 109: pikcha/Shutterstock; Ed Quinn/Corbis
Page 110: Dundanim/Shutterstock; Anton Ivanov/Shutterstock
Pages 112–113: michal812/Shutterstock; XuRa/Shutterstock; John Warburton-Lee/Getty Images
Page 114: amst/Shutterstock
Page 115: Cromagnon/Shutterstock; Viktorus/Shutterstock
Pages 116–117: Yuri Yavnik/Shutterstock
Page 118: Galyna Andrushko/Shutterstock; David Sutherland/Getty Images
Page 119: Pocholo Calapre/Shutterstock
Pages 120–121: Dale Wilson/Photographer's Choice RF/Getty Images; James P. Blair/National Geographic/Getty Images
Page 122: worradirek/Shutterstock; FloridaStock/Shutterstock; PSD photography/Shutterstock
Page 123: Mikhail Kolesnikov/Shutterstock
Pages 124–25: Dudarev Mikhail/Shutterstock; GNNick/Shutterstock; Anna Kucherova/Shutterstock; Manamana/Shutterstock (2); Fabio Lamanna/Shutterstock; Yoshikazu Tsuno/AFP/Getty Images; Tom Cockrem/Photolibrary/Getty Images
Page 126: Galyna Andrushko/Shutterstock
Page 127: Dan Ballard/Aurora/Getty Images
Page 128: Gorich/Shutterstock
Page 130: Catalin Petolea/Shutterstock
Page 131: Sebastian Kaulitzki/Shutterstock (2); CLIPAREA/Shutterstock (2)
Page 132: Sebastian Kaulitzki/Shutterstock
Page 133: Creative Commons; Anatomical Travelogue/Science Source/Getty Images
Page 134: maga/Shutterstock, Capital Pictures
Page 135: PathDoc/Shutterstock; Lightspring/Shutterstock
Pages 136–137: Andrea Danti/Shutterstock
Page 138: EcoPrint/Shutterstock; Robert Harding/IndiaPicture
Page 139: Sebastian Kaulitzki/Shutterstock
Page 140: Kiselev Andrey Valerevich/Shutterstock
Page 141: sciencepics/Shutterstock
Page 142: Fer Gregory/Shutterstock; sciencepics/Shutterstock
Page 143: Felix Mizioznikov/Dreamstime; Olga Popova / Shutterstock
Page 144: Juan Gaertner/Shutterstock
Page 145: Jochen Schoenfeld/Shutterstock; Blacqbook/Shutterstock; Sebastian Kaulitzki/Shutterstock
Page 146: chrupka/Shutterstock; Andrey Kuzmin/Shutterstock
Page 147: luminaimages/Shutterstock
Page 148: 2bears/Shutterstock
Page 150: Andrey Kuzmin/Shutterstock
Page 151: Yongyut Kumsri/Shutterstock
Pages 152–153: topseller/Shutterstock; UniversalImagesGroup/Getty Images; AP Photo/San Pedro News Pilot; John B. Carnett/Popular Science/Getty Images
Pages 154–155: Dudarev Mikhail/Shutterstock; Adek Berry/AFP/Getty Images; Evening Standard/Getty Images
Pages 156–157: Festa/Shutterstock; NASA (2)
Pages 158–159: Bulbash/Shutterstock; Vladitto/Shutterstock; steamroller_blues/Shutterstock
Page 160: Natursports/Shutterstock
Page 161: jules2000/Shutterstock
Pages 162–163: Christian Petersen-Clausen/Getty Images; Courtesy of Transrapid USA (2)
Pages 164–165: Kalmatsuy/Shutterstock; Mondadori Portfolio/Getty Images; Marka/Alamy/IndiaPicture
Pages 166–167: muratart/Shutterstock; Historic Florida/Alamy/India Picture
Pages 168–169: R. Gino Santa Maria/Shutterstock
Pages 170–171: Mark Harris/The Image Bank/Getty Images; Hulton Archive/Getty Images
Page 172: Jorg Hackemann/Shutterstock
Page 173: John Shearer/Invision/AP
Pages 174–175: kan khampanya/Shutterstock; AFP/Getty Images
Page 176: Hattanas Kumchai/Shutterstock; Timothy A. Clary/AFP/Getty Images
Page 177: Julie Clopper/Shutterstock; John Bryson/The LIFE Images Collection/Getty Images
Page 178: JP Jazz Archive/Redferns/Getty Images
Page 179: leoks/Shutterstock; NY Daily News/Getty Images
Page 180: Stuart Monk/Shutterstock
Page 181: cosma/Shutterstock; Universal Images Group/Getty Images
Page 182: Massimiliano Pieraccin/Shutterstock; Hulton Archive/Getty Images
Page 183: Frank Whitney/The Image Bank/Getty Images; Bloomberg/Getty Images
Page 184: Hulton Archive/Getty Images; Snap/Rex Features
Page 185: Charles Trainor/The LIFE Images Collection/Getty Images

WHY? WHO?
HERE? WHEN
OW? WHAT?
WHY? WHO?
HERE? WHEN
OW? WHAT?
WHY? WHO?
HERE? WHE
OW? WHAT?